50 WAYS TO A BETTER-LOOKING LAYOUT

Jeff Wilson

KALMBACH BOOKS

Kalmbach Books
21027 Crossroads Circle
Waukesha, Wisconsin 53186
www.Kalmbach.com/Books

© 2013 Kalmbach Books
All rights reserved. This book may not be reproduced in part or in
whole by any means whether electronic or otherwise without written
permission of the publisher except for brief excerpts for review.

Published in 2013
18 17 16 15 14   2 3 4 5 6

Manufactured in the United States of America

ISBN: 978-0-89024-819-5

Editor: Randy Rehberg
Art Director: Tom Ford

Some projects in this book originally appeared as articles in *Model Railroader* magazine.
Most have been edited and modified from their original form. The authors of these items
are indicated with each project.

Unless noted, photographs were taken by Jeff Wilson.

Publisher's Cataloging-In-Publication Data

Wilson, Jeff, 1964-
    50 ways to a better-looking layout / Jeff Wilson.

    p. : col. ill. ; cm. -- (Model railroader books) -- (Modeling & painting series)

    "Some projects in this book originally appeared as articles in Model Railroader
magazine."--T.p. verso.
    ISBN: 978-0-89024-819-5

    1. Railroads--Models--Handbooks, manuals, etc. 2. Models and modelmaking--
Handbooks, manuals, etc. I. Title. II. Title: Fifty ways to a better-looking layout
III. Series: Model railroader books.

TF197 .W557 2013
625.1/9

Contents

Introduction

Too many modelers rush to finish their layouts, losing sight of the fact that this hobby is not a race: it's a journey. Remember that a model railroad is never truly finished. There are always details to add, scenes to finish, and freight cars to weather. You can go back and redo scenes that have become dated, swap in new structures that reflect improved modeling skills, and upgrade locomotives and rolling stock.

This book highlights 50 different projects that feature a variety of techniques and ideas that you can use to improve your model railroad, regardless of its level of completion. Projects range from scenery and structures to locomotives, rolling stock, and details. Although a few of them are scale-specific, based on the availability of certain products, most are applicable for any scale.

Don't feel that you have to complete any of these projects by following steps line-by-line to get the same results I did. Instead, view them as ideas—starting points you can use as inspiration to personalize your own projects that fit the era, theme, and prototype of your layout.

Most of the projects in this book are composed of original material, but some have been taken from the pages of *Model Railroader* magazine. I thank the authors for completing these projects, and their names are listed at the end of each project.

I hope you enjoy the book and are inspired to try some new ideas and techniques for improving the appearance of your model railroad.

Convert a boxcar to a shed

This retired Athearn HO boxcar has found new life as a storage shed next to a yard.

Remove the car's cast-on steps and any underbody details that would prevent it from sitting on the ground.

To weather the car, I add oil-paint rust streaks on the sides and dark gray chalk grime on the roof and sides.

Add coarse ground foam to blend the car with the scenery and add detail items to complete the scene.

Old rolling stock is often retired and cut up for scrap, but sometimes cars find new life in other uses. One common practice is to convert a retired boxcar into a storage building.

Newer cars can also be converted if they've been damaged in a wreck. I chose an Athearn Ready-To-Roll car that had sustained some real-life damage in a nosedive off my workbench. I first removed the trucks, couplers, and molded-on stirrup steps.

Weather the car to make it look like it has been in service. I used artist's oil paints to give the car some rust streaks (pages 90–91) and followed with some chalk weathering on the roof and sides (pages 86–87). Then, seal the weathering with a light coat of clear flat finish.

Next, plant the car in an appropriate spot, usually at the edge of a yard or near a depot or maintenance building. I added some white glue to a level area and then set the car. Use ground foam to blend the car into the scenery.

My car is planted near a small yard, with a gravel access road (fine tan ballast) in front of it. I added a few 55-gallon drums (JL Innovative Design), a wheelbarrow (Con-Cor), and a small junk pile (Woodland Scenics). A Preiser figure completed the scene.

Detail an industrial loading dock

Adding interior and exterior details around a loading dock greatly improves the appearance of any structure. This is an HO warehouse built with DPM modular wall sections.

Adding details to the loading docks of industrial structures provides viewers with a clue regarding the products handled or produced, and also helps you set the theme and purpose of a layout.

Many models include the loading dock itself, but I added one to an HO scale brick building made from Design Preservation Models modular wall sections. I built the loading dock using .040" sheet styrene and painted it Polly Scale concrete. It's sized to match the height of the bottom of the door openings on the building and

long enough to serve two freight cars on a rail spur.

Consider what the business is handling and what the likely loads would be. Too many modelers add a random mix of wood crates, barrels, and sacks, without considering what would logically appear. Since the 1930s, most consumer products have been shipped in cardboard boxes.

My structure represents a grocery wholesaler in the 1960s. This means that the trackside loading dock will primarily serve inbound cars (mainly insulated and standard boxcars) of

The roll-up doors are simulated by gluing pieces of corrugated sheet styrene inside the door opening.

The shadow box is made from .060" styrene. Make it large enough to fit behind the openings in the structure.

The artwork for the Campbell's cases was made as described on pages 8–9. The printout is glued to a wood block.

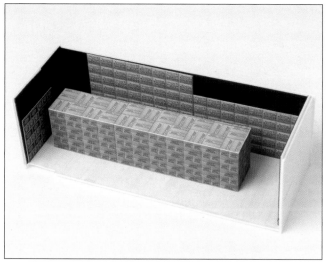

The finished shadow box has a mix of 3-D stacks of cases as well as other case artwork glued to the walls.

Here's the shadow box from behind, glued in place in the structure.

products, most of which will be shipped in cardboard cases. By the 1960s, pallets were commonly used, making it easier for crews to handle loads with forklifts and hand trucks. If you model an earlier period, you can feature hand-stacked piles of cases.

Opening the structure doors at the dock and adding some interior details make a huge impact on the appearance of a building. You don't need to add interior detail to the entire structure. By fitting a small shadow box behind the doors, you can give the appearance of a lot more detail than is actually there. This is a technique you can use with any type of structure including storefronts, railroad stations, and houses.

The original DPM building had heavy cast doors. I replaced these with corrugated roll-up doors, simulated by gluing pieces of corrugated styrene in each opening.

Build a shadow box to fit your structure. Mine spans two entrance doors. It's made from .060" styrene sheet. The floor is painted Polly Scale concrete, and the walls are black mat board glued into place. (The black walls help hide the lack of depth.) The walls should be tall enough so viewers can't see over them.

I made the stacks of cardboard boxes as explained on pages 8–9. I wound up with cases of Del Monte vegetables, Campbell's Pork and Beans, and Sunshine Krispy Crackers.

I made large sections of the Campbell's cases and glued the resulting printout to a wood block. This provided a 3-D appearance directly behind the doors. I glued the block in place and added flat printouts of the Del Monte and Sunshine cases to the walls of the shadow box. I then glued the box in place behind the door openings.

You can finish the dock itself with additional stacks of cases and other details. My scene has a Kibri forklift, a hand cart from an old Con-Cor detail set, and several Preiser figures.

In addition to making your own cases and loads, you can use commercial items. Bar Mills, Preiser, Heljan, JL Innovative Design, Kibri, and others make a huge variety of cases, barrels, and other items.

Cardboard cases by the stack

A forklift driver prepares to unload a pallet of cardboard boxes from a Western Pacific boxcar in this HO scale scene. The stack is glued atop a Preiser pallet.

From the 1930s onward, cardboard cartons became the preferred method of packaging canned goods and other consumer products. These often feature distinctive logos and lettering. With a bit of photo-editing knowledge, you can make stacks of these cases in short order.

Start by getting photos of the boxes you want to duplicate. I used a Del Monte canned-fruit carton. I took photos of several cases at antique stores and from my own collection, and I also found photos of many cartons online. It helps to have photos of a side, the

end, and the top of the carton. Scan or import these images to your computer.

Using Photoshop Elements, I corrected the perspective of each view with the program's skew tool and created separate images for the carton's side, end, and top. I then created a blank Photoshop document and dropped in the side, end, and top views. Then it was a matter of resizing each to match the proper scale (HO for this project), duplicating each item, and arranging the pieces.

I made some pallet-sized stacks, some larger stacks suitable for warehouses, and some single cases. Print the

Take or find photos of the box that you wish to model. Depending upon the photo's angle, you may have to correct the angles so the final images are rectangular.

Place copies of the end, side, and top artwork together in the proper scale. The alternating end and top views reflect an alternating stacking pattern.

Print out the artwork on matte photo paper. Several items will fit on a single sheet of paper.

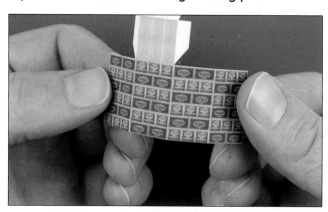

Cut out the stack. The tabs on the top make it easy to glue the mating corners to each other.

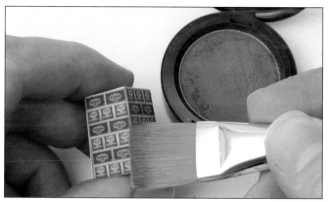

Hide the white corners by touching up the areas with a soft brush and the appropriate color chalk or makeup.

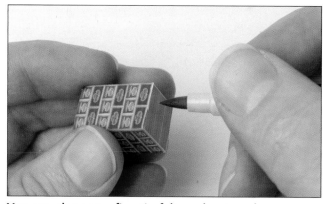

You can also use a fine-tip felt marker to color any exposed white paper areas.

results on matte photo paper or thin cardstock.

Trim each stack, leaving flaps along each mating edge so the sides can be easily glued together. Use a hobby knife to lightly score the face along each line that must be folded. You can also glue the artwork to a solid block of wood.

The folds will show an unrealistic area of white that you can get rid by brushing appropriately colored chalk on the seam. Chalk works well because it sticks in the seam but can be brushed off the faces. (You can also use makeup. I have a few mica-free makeup cases on hand for weathering.) If you use fine-tip felt markers, you need to be very precise to avoid marking the surfaces.

These cases can be used in warehouses, loading docks, freight cars, trucks, stores, station platforms, and other suitable places.

A NOTE ON COPYRIGHT

You can use images and items with corporate trademarks (such as these) for your own modeling purposes, but you cannot legally distribute them (whether or not you charge money for them) to others without permission of the trademark holders. Likewise, you can't distribute images from photos of others without their permission.

Signs out of matchbooks

Matchbooks supplied the artwork for the large Super Valu storefront sign and most of the window signs, including Red Cup Coffee, 7up, Sealtest Ice Cream, and two for Hansen's bread.

Period signs and logos can help set the era of a scene or layout, and a great way to get signs that aren't available commercially is to make your own using artwork from matchbook covers.

Especially from the early through mid-1900s, matchbooks were a common advertising giveaway item for national companies as well as local businesses. Matchbooks provide a wealth of logos and lettering for potential business signs for products and businesses. I've found most of mine in antique stores, and you can find them on eBay as well.

Using personal computers and photo-editing software, it's easy to turn a matchbook into a sign of any size. (It's OK to scan items with trademarked logos for your own use, but selling or distributing them is not allowed.)

The first step is to scan the cover and import it to your computer. Scan the covers at 300 dpi or higher resolution for best results.

You can then take logos, lettering, and other elements from the scans to make your signs using photo-editing software such as Photoshop Elements. I made two separate signs from one Hansen's

Matchbooks can be found with a wide variety of logos, artwork, and lettering.

This screen shot from Photoshop Elements shows how I cleaned the background and rotated the logo for the Colonial bread sign (top). You can also see how I used half of the Hansen's matchbook to make one sign.

Along with window signs, this sheet shows several large building signs made by combining matchbook logos with computer lettering.

For window signs, apply gloss medium to the sign face with a toothpick.

Press the sign in place on the clear plastic glazing. The gloss medium will dry clear and won't be noticeable.

You can also use matchbook covers to make freestanding signs. I cut out this 7up sign and mounted it on a simple, stained stripwood frame with two legs.

bread matchbook. One is a poster with lettering only; the other uses the loaf artwork. Stains and imperfections can be fixed with the cloning tool, and you can expand and alter backgrounds.

Once you're done editing, the signs can be resized. I like to print out signs in multiple sizes onto matte photo paper.

Use a scissors or sharp hobby knife and a straightedge to cut them out.

Window signs can be cut out and glued directly to clear styrene glazing. Apply gloss medium to the face of the sign and press it to the glazing. The milky color of the gloss medium will disappear as it dries.

Larger signs can be fixed to .020" or thicker styrene sheets and mounted directly to structures, such as the Kann's Market sign. You can also make freestanding signs by adding a simple stripwood frame and a couple of legs, or you can make a large billboard (see pages 30–31).

3-D signs from stir sticks

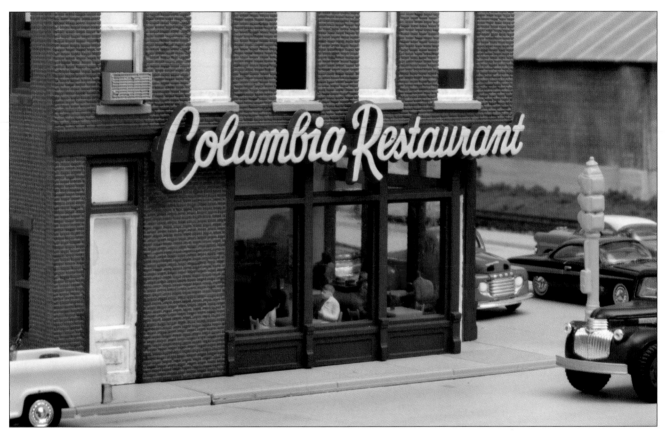

The Columbia Restaurant lettering on this HO scale Design Preservation Models structure came directly from a plastic stir stick. All I needed to do was trim the stick and glue the lettering in place.

Among the best ways of personalizing a structure is to give it a unique sign, and a sign with 3-D lettering draws attention to a structure. Plastic stir sticks, or swizzle sticks, are one of the best sources for unique raised lettering.

Stir sticks have been produced in countless styles for a variety of businesses including restaurants, bars, clubs, airlines, hotels, and amusement parks. Some are from popular national chains, while others advertise lesser-known, local businesses.

The key is finding a stir stick having raised lettering that can be trimmed from the stick. The lettering can be used as is, or individual letters can be trimmed and rearranged to form new words and business names. Along with the lettering, other symbols and shapes can be used in signs.

My examples are all in HO scale, but many stir sticks have lettering in sizes that would work in N, S, and O scales as well.

Trimming the letters is usually best done with a razor saw. Work slowly and keep the blade as flat as possible

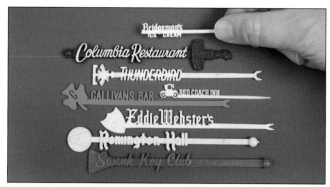

Look for stir sticks with raised lettering in various styles. The longer the names, the more you can do by rearranging the letters.

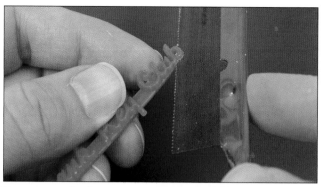

To remove the letters, cut them carefully with a razor saw, keeping the blade as flat as possible against the stick.

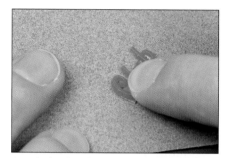

Sand the backs of the letters flat and remove plastic flash by rubbing them on 220 grit sandpaper.

Here's the finished Club portion of the sign cut from the Swank Key Club stir stick.

The letters can be glued to styrene signboards, such as this one made from Evergreen tile styrene sheet.

I sized the signboard to fit above the door and windows of this Smalltown U.S.A. brick building, which became the Key Club.

The Bridgeman's Ice Cream sign is another example of a stir stick that was simply trimmed and glued to a building.

against the stir stick so that all letters and letter groups have a uniform thickness. You can smooth out the backs by rubbing letters on medium (220 grit) sandpaper or a fine, flat mill file. Remove any remaining plastic burrs with a sharp hobby knife. The finished lettering will be quite clean.

You can mount the lettering directly to a building or glue it to a signboard first. Styrene sheet, including plain or tile sheets, works well for creating a signboard. On my Key Club sign, I secured the letters with liquid plastic cement, but cyanoacrylate adhesive adheres well with various plastics. For glue compatibility, test it on a scrap piece of the stir stick.

The lettering can often be left on the stick, with the stick trimmed at each end. The Columbia Restaurant and Bridgeman's Ice Cream signs are both examples of this. There are thousands of ways that signs can be mounted—look at period photos and real-world examples for inspiration.

Stir sticks are molded in many colors, and can sometimes be used without having to paint them. The Columbia stick was already two colors: the molded blue with painted white on the lettering. Unpainted plastic looks similar to large molded prototype signs. You can also paint the signs, and airbrushing works best to provide an even appearance.

I've found most of my stir sticks in antique stores, rarely paying more than a dollar apiece for them. You can also find them on eBay and from other sources. Keep your eyes open, and you'll soon have a city full of truly unique structures.

Advertising sign decals

The Dr. Pepper sign adds a bit of color to this HO downtown scene. Although it's a decal, the sign appears to be painted on the structure.

Downtown brick buildings through the mid-1900s served as canvases for large billboard-style advertising signs. Even today, many of these signs survive (albeit quite weathered), sometimes promoting brands and products that haven't existed for decades. Re-creating one of these signs with a decal adds character to any city or town scene.

I decided to add a decal sign to an HO brick structure from Walthers that I had already painted and detailed. With care, the decal will snuggle into the brick surface and appear to be painted on the wall.

Microscale makes a variety of suitable decals in all scales. I chose a Dr. Pepper sign from an O scale decal set (48-625). A tip here is that, when it comes to signs, the scale listed on the package doesn't matter.

To apply, first cut the decal as close to the artwork as possible using a sharp hobby knife and a straightedge.

Cut the sign from the decal sheet as close to the artwork as possible with a sharp knife and a straightedge.

Slide the decal from the backing sheet onto a puddle of Micro-Set on the building surface.

Carefully slice any air bubbles or areas where the decal didn't settle into the grooves of the brickwork. Use a light touch with the knife.

Use a soft brush to reapply some Micro-Sol liberally to the entire surface of the decal. The decal should then settle into the surface.

I lightly weathered the wall and sign with some dark red chalk, as I wanted the sign to appear fairly new.

Then dip the decal in distilled water. (Mineral deposits in tap water will leave residue when the decal dries.) While it's soaking, paint a large puddle of Microscale Micro-Set on the wall where the decal will go. This will help soften the decal so it nestles into the brickwork.

After sliding the decal from its backing paper onto the building, use a soft brush to adjust the decal into the position you want it in. When it's in place, let the decal set for a few minutes. Then use a brush to add Microscale Micro-Sol (a stronger setting solution than Micro-Set) around its edges. Capillary action will draw the Micro-Sol under the surface. Leave the decal alone until it is dry.

Poke any air bubbles with a hobby knife and slit any areas that didn't settle into the molded brickwork. Reapply Micro-Sol generously to the entire decal and let it dry. This should make the entire decal settle into the surface, but repeat the process if any bubbles remain.

Weather the wall and sign as desired. I faded the sign a bit by brushing on some dark red chalk (a shade close in color to the wall), sealed it with clear flat spray, and then applied light gray chalk over the entire wall, which settled into the cracks like mortar. Once the appearance was what I was looking for, I applied another light coat of clear flat finish to seal it. You can vary the weathering, depending on if you're modeling a recent sign or an older one.

Give buildings a level base

Structures such as this HO plaster model should appear to be firmly planted in the ground.

A big step in transforming a collection of models into a model railroad is to make sure that all of the structures look like they are part of the scenery. A building that merely sits on the ground, with a gap under a wall, instantly makes a scene look toylike and unrealistic.

In most cases, this is easy to fix. For my example, I'm using an HO warehouse structure built from a cast-plaster kit by C.C. Crow. You can apply the same techniques to almost any structure regardless of scale.

First, make sure that the building has a firm, level base. The structure in the photos sits on a base of cork roadbed that's glued to the layout surface. If you're adding a building to a finished scene, use a piece of foam core, gator board, or thin plywood as a base, building the scenery up to it, before adding the structure.

For my building, the scenery was completed to the cork base. However, the structure was merely sitting on the pad, and appeared to be almost floating above the ground foam scenery.

To fix this, I ran a bead of Woodland Scenics Scenic Cement along

Each building must have a firm, level base. This building rests on a base of cork roadbed that's glued to the plywood layout surface.

A structure that appears to "float" above the ground like this one has a toylike appearance.

To eliminate the floating, first run a bead of Woodland Scenics Scenic Cement along the structure's base.

Then apply coarse ground foam to hide the gap where the structure meets its base and the scenery.

On the rail side of the building, I added the same ballast used for the track, brushing it up to the structure.

To glue the ballast in place, start by soaking it with rubbing alcohol applied with an eyedropper or pipette.

Add diluted white glue to the ballast. The alcohol ensures that the glue spreads throughout the ballast.

The finished building appears to be part of the scenery.

the base of the wall and then pressed clumps of coarse green ground foam into the glue. This glue dries clear and flat, and the building now looks like it's firmly in the ground.

You can do the same with other types of ground as well. On the rear side of the building, I brushed the same fine ballast/ground foam mix that I had used on the adjoining rail

spur against the building. I fixed it as I did the ballast by soaking it with rubbing alcohol followed by diluted white glue (one part glue to four parts water).

Improve roofs on structures

These HO structures from Bachmann, Walthers, and Design Preservation Models all received different roof treatments and details. You can use these techniques in any scale.

Roofs in real life tend to be out of sight. On layouts, however, we look down on our models, which makes structure roofs worthy of some extra attention. There are a number of things you can do to improve building roofs in any scale.

Start with the roof itself. Some structures have roofs that include texture and detail (the Bachmann drugstore at left in above photo). I painted this a mix of black and grimy black.

The roof on the Walthers building (at center of above photo) is molded in dark gray plastic, but it lacks detail. I

scribed lines across it with a dental pick to add roofing material seams.

Gaps between the roof and walls do not look good. I ran a bead of gap-filling cyanoacrylate adhesive (CA) around the roof edges of this building. This can also be done around vent pipes. When it dried, I brush-painted it black to look like roofing tar had been applied.

The Design Preservation Models corner building kit (at right in above photo) came with a plain piece of white styrene for a roof, so I took a different approach with it. Roofs made of tar topped with gravel or crushed rock were

Scribe seam marks across the roof with a dental pick, using a piece of styrene as a straightedge.

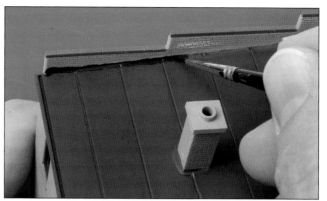

Fill gaps along the roof edge with thick CA and then brush-paint the filler material black to represent tar.

These plastic air-conditioning units and vents from Walthers are a few of the many roof details available.

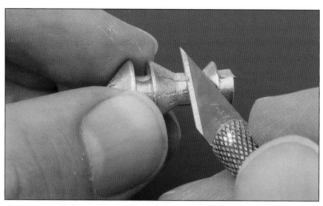

Cast-metal details, such as this 202 vent from Bar Mills, sometimes require cleanup with a knife or needle file.

Paint details in appropriate colors (silver for the vent pipes) and glue them in place.

Solid chimneys can be improved by adding a brass-tube chimney pipe.

common through the 1960s. I modeled this by giving the roof a heavy coat of black paint and then sprinkling fine ballast on it (a mix of cinders and gray).

Some structures include a smokestack, vents, and other details, but you can also add your own. Walthers has a number of detail sets for roofs, including vents (933-3158) and air conditioners (933-3157)—a small one is mounted on the DPM building. Bar Mills, Gold Medal Models, Great West Models, Rix,

Tichy, and others also offer roof details. Many can be used in multiple scales depending on the size of the structure.

The Walthers building included a chimney, and I added a vent pipe with a cap, a metal casting from Bar Mills (204). Metal details, such as the Bar Mills vent, sometimes need a bit of cleanup. When completed, paint the details appropriate colors and glue them in place, either in mounting holes or on the roof surface.

On the DPM building, I added chimney pipes by drilling ⅛" holes into the chimneys and inserting short lengths of brass tubing painted black. I also added a couple of brass-tube vent stacks toward the rear of the roof.

Weathering goes a long way toward finishing a realistic roof. Here, I used chalks, as described on pages 86–87. I gave the chimneys a lot of attention with black chalk and used dark gray and black to streak the roofs in various areas.

Build cardstock structures

Photos by Richard Bohlman

Richard Bohlman built this HO scale freight house and retaining wall from cardstock kits that he downloaded from supplier websites and printed.

Building HO, N, and O scale models from cardstock has often been overlooked here in the United States, but it has a long and popular history in Europe. Cardstock models were once only available as printed kits and texture sheets, but the growth of the Internet has led to a wide variety of printable kits including buildings, tunnels, retaining walls, streets, shops, and signs.

After buying a kit, the product is supplied either as a download or a CD that is mailed to you (and some are available for free). Digital cardstock kits are typically supplied in PDF (Portable Document Format), which allows you to download, open, view, and print each page.

One benefit of a cardstock model is that if you make a mistake while building the kit, you can simply reprint the part needed and continue building. You also have the potential to build a kit as many times as you like, or you can customize the kit to suit your layout by altering its height and length. This is a big advantage when scratchbuilding or undertaking large construction projects. Also, many

With a basic selection of tools and kit printouts, you're ready to start building. If you make a mistake, you can just print another kit.

This is just a small selection of some of the HO scratchbuilding sheets available from cardstock suppliers. Sheets are also available in other scales.

of these kits feature detailed interiors and include tips to enhance the overall appearance of the completed structure.

Typical cardstock structures have a high level of photo-quality detail. No painting is required—just cut, glue, and position it on your layout. You can get a good feel for cardstock modeling by starting with one of the many free models that can be downloaded online. The small freight house pictured is from Scalescenes.com. It includes illustrated instructions, which makes it a good starter kit for beginners.

The complexity of the models ranges from beginner to advanced. For the advanced modeler looking for a challenge, these models allow for flexibility and creativity. For the novice modeler, each kit supplies thorough step-by-step directions, and illustrations are typically provided to guide you through the building process.

For scratchbuilders, online cardstock suppliers such as Scalescenes.com and Clever Models are a real gold mine. They provide a wide range

of realistic texture sheets in common model railroad scales.

Another scratchbuilding option is using Model Builder software from Evan Designs. This program lets you position walls, windows, doors, and trim on your computer screen. You can then print the walls for easy assembly.

To build cardstock structures, you'll need several tools and some basic supplies. A hobby knife with a sharp blade works well for cutting, but be sure to change the blade regularly as paper dulls knives quickly. When cutting, a cutting mat and a metal straightedge prevent the blade from wandering.

Use a glue stick to attach sheets to paper without wrinkles. Cyanoacrylate adhesive is great for quickly applying sheets to plastic, and white glue is the best choice when using wood.

You'll need tweezers for placing small components and sandpaper sheets and sanding sticks for smoothing edges.

Fine-tip felt markers in gray and brown tones are handy for coloring any

white edges. You can also use artist's soft pastel chalks to blend black or brown tones on a sheet of paper and then rub the powder into the corners and joints of a model with a soft brush. A clear matte overspray will protect and seal the cardstock.

—*Richard Bohlman*

ONLINE MODEL SOURCES

Scalescenes.com
(rail structures, town buildings, and textures)

Clever Models
clevermodels.net
(structure kits and textures)

Evan Designs
modeltrainsoftware.com
(software for many paper buildings)

IGS Hansa
igshansa.de/igsorg
(This German website offers container downloads in English.)

Impressionistic interiors

Photos by Michael Tylic

Saulena's Tavern appears to be a lively watering hole. Actually, there's less going on inside than meets the eye.

Empty model buildings, especially those in the foreground, look like abandoned shells when large windows reveal empty rooms. I've developed some quick and simple techniques for interiors that can withstand the scrutiny of foreground placement. The techniques used here for my O scale structures can be applied to buildings of any scale.

For the upstairs rooms of Saulena's Tavern, I cut pieces of scrap mat board, colored them with markers, and taped them where they would be visible through the windows. When I was satisfied with their placement, I glued them in place. They're brightly colored and impressionistic. They really don't need to be accurately rendered—the shape shows that something is there, and viewers' imaginations fill in the rest.

I tend to cover all surfaces that could be seen by a viewer. The building interior, when viewed without the roof, appears cluttered, but when seen through the windows, it just looks inhabited. Curtains and shades made from pieces of paper and cloth scraps add detail while obscuring the lack of interior detail.

The building's interior proves that less is more. Brightly colored walls, floors, and furnishings suggest that the upstairs is inhabited.

Through the upstairs windows, you can see that the walls are painted, curtains adorn the windows, and furniture seems to be available for family and friends.

The tavern walls are drawn freehand, and the tables and chairs are made of cardstock and stripwood. The figures are not foreground quality and belong inside.

The bakery features potted plants made of plastic tubing and foliage clusters and other interior details cut from photo printouts.

The hanging clothes visible inside Like Nu Cleaners were cut from photos taken at a real dry cleaner.

I used markers to paint the walls, sometimes adding patterns to suggest wallpaper. I also drew pieces of art hanging on the walls and sketched a floor lamp on one wall. Representations of area rugs cover some of the floors, and black marker lines suggest floorboards.

In the tavern downstairs, I drew booths and a door on one wall. The bar is simply a few scrap pieces of mat board glued together. The beer taps are bits of wire with insulation left on the ends to represent handles. For plates, I used markers to color disks of paper (paper-punch scraps). Sitting on the plates are glasses made from short lengths of plastic tubing. Bits of paper and a few beads suggest items on the tables.

The interior of Cimura's Bakery features some potted plants. A few short lengths of plastic tubing, a little terra-cotta paint, and Woodland Scenics foliage clusters did the job. The bakery's cash register is a small block of wood colored black. Remember that impressions are all we're looking for—you're simply trying to fool the viewer into thinking something is there that really isn't.

The tile on the floor in Saulena's Tavern and the "carpet tile" floor in the dry cleaner's shop are computer generated. Using almost any photo or drawing program, you can produce a pattern of alternating colored squares. I also used my computer to make wall and window signs and wainscoting for several buildings.

I experimented with photographic interiors for the cleaners and the bakery. I scaled the photos in Adobe Photoshop and printed them on photo paper. Instead of trying to get one perfect background image, I took lots of shots. Then I pasted the photos on cardstock and cut out the details I needed.

The hanging clothes and items on the counter at Like Nu Cleaners are cut from photos. I also photographed signs, cut them out, and glued them to the windows.

The photographed bread on the bakery fixtures looks almost good enough to eat. I also glued a photo of some bakery racks to a back wall to create the illusion of a back room that can be seen through the open doorway. This is only a half-inch or so from the first rear wall, but it gives an illusion of depth.

You get the idea. On a layout, these buildings simply appear to be lived in—exactly the look you're after.

—*Michael Tylic*

Scratchbuilt exhaust fans

Bruce Dombey added easy-to-scratchbuild exhaust fans to several structures on his O scale layout.

The four parts of the fan are the inner tube, outer case, square base, and cap. By varying the depth, you can create different versions of the fan. *Photos by Bruce Dombey*

I wanted to upgrade some of the structures on my O scale layout, and it occurred to me that wall- or roof-mounted exhaust fans would be an appropriate detail for many different businesses and industries. In fact, any enclosed industrial or commercial space where emissions might be hazardous or potent uses an exhaust fan.

The fan I modeled was based on a real fan used to exhaust the cooking area of a carry-out restaurant that specialized in roasted chicken. This fan was 24" in diameter, 18" deep, and had a 27" x 27" base.

I have built many versions of this fan. Each time, I maintained the diameter and base sizes, but I varied the depth in 3-scale-inch increments from 9" to 18" to suit different applications.

Each fan is made from four parts of Evergreen styrene: the inner tube, outer case, square base, and cap. I made the outer case from ½"-diameter tubing and cut each one to the same length. I cut the base from .030" thick sheet using a standard ¼"-diameter hole punch. You can vary the dimensions based on your modeling scale and the type of installation.

I centered the outer case on the base and cemented it in place using Ambroid Pro Weld. I then centered the inner tube in the outer case and bonded it to the base. I centered the cap and attached it to the inner tube.

I also added nut-bolt-washer castings to further detail the bases, and then painted the fans to blend in with the structures.

—*Bruce Dombey*

Show vehicles turning

The angled front wheel on this Classic Metal Works HO Dodge Meadowbrook makes it apparent that the vehicle is making a right-hand turn at this intersection.

Start by removing the front wheel and tire from the axle. A small screwdriver often does the trick.

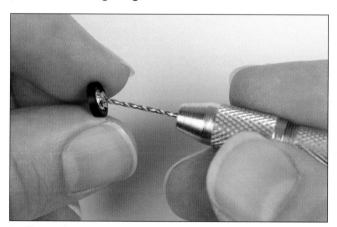

Drill out the mounting hole to create a slot at a 45-degree angle. Work slowly and carefully.

Glue the wheel back in place. Make sure that the wheel itself is vertical when installed.

The appearance of a vehicle turning, with the front wheels at an angle, adds a touch of realism to a street scene. You can do this to almost any model that uses separate plastic wheel and tire assemblies mounted to wire axles.

First, remove the front wheels from the axle. Some easily pull off using fingers; others need to be pried off with a

screwdriver. You can model both wheels turning or do just one, which gives you the option of placing the vehicle in either a straight or turning position.

Using a pin vise with a drill bit that matches the axle diameter, carefully ream the axle hole in the wheel and create a slot in the original hole at about a 45-degree angle. Be sure you don't drill through the wheel.

Place a dot of cyanoacrylate adhesive on the end of the axle and glue the wheel back in place. Gluing the axle in place ensures that the wheel stays in the proper position. If you do both wheels, take care to see that both wheels are mounted in the same relative position. Make sure the finished wheels remain vertical and are not canted, or leaning outward or inward.

Detail sidewalk scenes

This HO scene includes these realistic details: a highway sign (Blair Line 108), Coke machine (SS Ltd. 2405), parking meter (Walthers 933-3535), mailbox (Walthers 933-3535), and Preiser figures.

Adding an assortment of details to your town and city sidewalk scenes helps make your model railroad come alive and seem like a place where people live and work. Figures are a great start, as explained on pages 34–35, but there are dozens of other great details you can add.

Highway signs are a must. In towns, they are often mounted on light or utility poles, or they can be seen on their own posts. Blair Line makes a wide variety of them in N, HO, and O scales. These include route signs as well as speed limit, parking, stop, yield, and other regulatory signs.

City scenes are naked without streetlights and stoplights. Nonoperating cast-metal versions are shown from Woodland Scenics set 248; you can also add operating models from

This corner features several figures, Blair Line signs mounted on a Woodland Scenics lamppost, and an Athearn Coke machine.

Other popular city details include a Walthers phone booth, Woodland Scenics stoplight, and a Blair Line highway sign on a wooden post.

Miniatronics, Walthers, and other manufacturers.

Vending machines are common in front of service stations and in various sidewalk locations. You can see samples of Scale Structures Ltd. (2405) and Athearn Coca-Cola machines in the photos.

Fire hydrants are found in almost every town and city. The one pictured is from American Model Builders (404).

A great start in HO scale is the Walthers city accessory package (933-3535), which features popular injection-molded details. The photos show a parking meter, mailbox, and phone booth from the kit. The kit also includes trash cans, fire hydrants, and bicycle racks.

Keep your eyes open in real life (as well as in hobby shops) for potential details to add.

This American Model Builders fire hydrant is a common city detail.

Roadway striping and weathering

Road markings on this HO scene include white dashed stripes, a yellow no-passing stripe on the road (at left), crosswalks, and parking lines.

Adding road markings improves the appearance of your streets and highways and also helps set the era of your model railroad. You can apply these with dry-transfer or decal stripes, but I chose paint for my 1960s city scene.

Which markings are appropriate depends upon the era you model. Today's yellow dashed center line (single or double solid yellow for no-passing areas) and white stripes for divided highways date to 1971. Before that, white dashed stripes were used, with solid yellow lines

on either side for no-passing zones. Solid striping along the road edges (fog lines) came into use in the 1950s.

The best source for information on markings is the *Manual on Uniform Traffic Control Devices* (mutcd.fhwa.dot. gov), published by the U.S. Government. Links to past issues of the MUTCD (dating back to the 1930s) can be found at trafficsign.us/oldmutcd.html.

Most dashed lines today on highways are about 10 feet long with 30-foot gaps; the 1961 MUTCD recommended 15-foot stripes with 25-foot gaps. Lines are 4" or 6" wide,

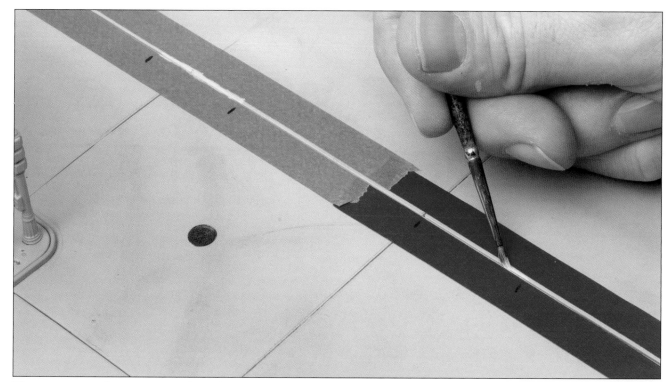

Place tape a scale 6" apart and mark dashed-line spacing on the tape. Brush-paint white or yellow paint smoothly to create the lines.

Crosswalks, parking lines, and other markings can be completed using the same techniques.

Chalk works well for weathering streets and highways. You can apply it with a brush or simply use your finger.

and the wide stop bars now used at intersections and railroad crossings are 24" wide.

To add, start by applying one piece of masking tape to define the edge of the stripe. Place a second piece of tape a scale 6" from the first. Press the tape edges firmly to avoid paint bleeding under. For dashed lines, mark the spacing on one piece of tape. Use a brush to paint the stripe—I used Polly Scale reefer white and reefer yellow. One coat is fine for older lines that are fading, but use two coats for new lines.

To paint multiple lines (such as the white stripes with a yellow no-passing line), use thin strips of tape between the lines. You can cut your own tape to width or use thin masking tape such as 3M Fine Line. Narrow tape also works well for curves.

Crosswalks and other markings are done in similar fashion. If any paint bleeds under the tape, touch it up with the pavement paint color.

Weathering roads also adds realism to a layout. I use either powdered chalk, applied with a stiff brush, or chalk rubbed on with a finger. To do

this, touch a finger to the chalk and then rub (begin lightly) along the road. A general gray streak down the middle of each lane looks good, with more-concentrated areas to simulate oil and fluid drippings where cars pause (intersections and parking spaces).

An advantage of weathering with chalk is that the chalk can be wiped off with a damp cloth if you don't like the effect. There's no real need to seal the chalk with a clear overcoat—as long as the initial paint on your streets is flat, it will hold the chalk just fine.

Set an era with roadside billboards

Billboards, such as this HO model, help set the era and mood of a model railroad.

Billboards sometimes seem to be everywhere in real life. They can be a colorful addition to a layout and help set the era of a model railroad by displaying era-appropriate graphics.

Billboards have two important parts: the frame and the graphics that go on the face of the board. Several companies make frames (usually offered with graphics), and most produce additional sign sheets.

I used an HO Athearn frame for the billboard shown above. They are available without graphics (933-3133),

but in the past, they have been offered with a variety of signs. The styrene kit is very easy to assemble—glue everything together with liquid plastic cement. I painted mine flat dark green.

You can generally use a paper or cardstock billboard from any manufacturer, but you might have to trim it to fit, as I did with the JL Innovative Coca-Cola sign. Use just a small dab of white glue in a few spots around the perimeter of the sign to hold it in place (double-sided tape also works).

A special billboard category is the laser-cut wood, open-frame style

A wide variety of billboard illustrations is available, including these HO auto billboards from JL Innovative Design and various N scale billboards from Blair Line.

You can use just about any graphic on any billboard frame by trimming the graphic to fit.

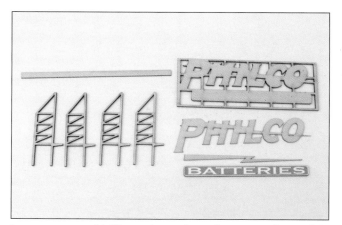

Laser-cut wood billboards, such as this Bar Mills model, feature fine three-dimensional detail.

Painting makes the laser-cut details stand out. Open-frame billboards are real eye-catchers.

The Pure road map at left became the basis for the billboard at right by using imaging software.

Installed on a hill, the Pure billboard lets HO drivers know a gas station (with OK'd rest rooms) is ahead.

offered in N through O scales by Bar Mills and Blair Line. These are easy to assemble and, once painted, become very distinctive models. They can be used as freestanding billboards or mounted atop buildings.

With these, paint every side of all the wood pieces to minimize warping.

Painting the frame components dark gray or black makes the brighter-colored artwork and signs stand out. I brush-painted everything on the Bar Mills Philco billboard, but using an airbrush makes some of the painting a bit easier.

You can also design or produce your own artwork. I made a Pure Oil

billboard based on artwork from a 1960s Pure road map. I scanned the artwork into my computer, corrected the perspective using Photoshop Elements, and printed out the results. The sign is glued to .020" styrene, with a simple stripwood frame stained black to support it.

Add locomotive cab crews

Adding a figure or two inside a locomotive cab is easy to do and will add life and realism to your layout. I easily inserted this Preiser figure in an HO Proto 1000 Alco RS-2.

You can add realism to a layout simply by adding crew members to your locomotive cabs. After all, it's rather disconcerting to see a locomotive leading a train down the tracks with an empty cab.

Preiser and other manufacturers offer a variety of painted scale figures in HO and other scales. You can also paint your own engineer figures (see pages 34–35). Don't worry about finding figures made specifically as engineers—almost any seated figure will work.

How you add figures depends upon the design of each model. Some loco-

motives include a cab interior, others have wide-open space for the cab, and some have only limited space between the side windows and chassis.

The Kato GP35 and Proto 2000 E8 have basic cab details. Remove their shell following the instructions, which will vary with each model. The Proto locomotive actually includes two figures, but everything is molded in black plastic. I substituted a seated Preiser figure instead, and then used a brush to give the interior a coat of light gray paint. For the Kato engine, I super-glued a seated figure to each cab seat.

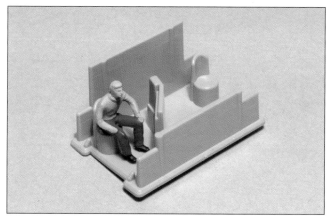

Kato's HO EMD models have a molded, basic cab interior that includes seats on each side of the cab.

Both figures are visible in this view looking through the Kato GP35.

The window glazing obscures the view enough that detailed interiors and figures aren't needed. This is an HO Proto 2000 E8.

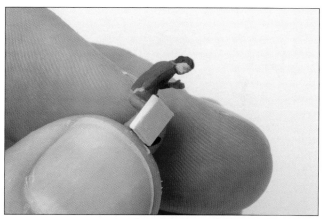

I prepped this Preiser figure for the cab of the Proto 1000 RS-2 by painting his shirt blue and gluing his legs to a piece of .060" styrene.

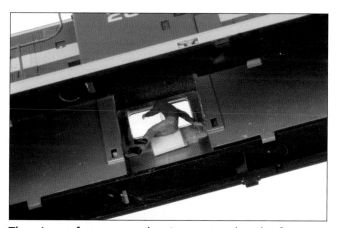

The piece of styrene makes it easy to glue the figure in place against the cab wall. I used clear parts cement since super glue can fog clear plastic.

You can open a cab window for a different look simply by omitting the glazing. The figure will be much more apparent.

Make sure you test-fit the figures—some cabs have limited headroom.

Other locomotives, such as the Proto 1000 Alco RS-2, don't have a cab interior. I added an engineer by gluing a figure to a piece of .060" styrene (to space it away from the wall) and then gluing the styrene to the side of the cab interior wall. Because the background is black, all you see is the figure behind the side window.

As views of the completed locomotives show, when looking through a plastic "glass" window or windshield, the lack of detail isn't apparent. The figures provide realism and make it seem like someone is in control of the train.

You can model an open window by leaving out the glazing. The engineer in the Illinois Central GP10 is simply glued to the cab wall as with the RS-2.

Paint your own figures

Several home-painted HO scale Preiser figures pose outdoors and indoors in this scene. It's easy and economical to paint your own figures.

Figures are key to making any model railroad scene look active and vibrant. Even a small layout can absorb hundreds of figures, which can put a dent in the wallet if you buy decorated figures. An inexpensive alternative is to buy unpainted figures and paint them yourself.

Before painting, remove any mold lines or imperfections with a hobby knife. If the figures are attached to sprues, leave them attached as the sprue serves as a painting handle.

Start by painting the skin color and then progressively add darker colors. For skin, try Polly Scale Flesh (32648) or Modelflex Light Flesh (16204) for caucasian skin, and Modelflex Dark Flesh (16206) or Medium Flesh (16205) for African-American or darker skin tones.

For clothing, I prefer using craft paints such as Delta Ceramcoat and Apple Barrel. These acrylics cover well, are easy to brush on, and come in a multitude of colors. Apply paint with a fine-tip (no. 0) brush, working colors up to clothing separation lines. Don't worry if you get paint where you don't want it—wait for it to dry and then touch it up. Solid colors are easiest to

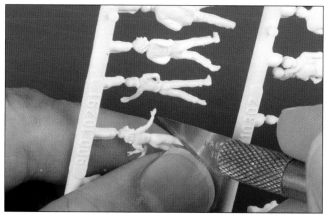

Clean up any mold parting lines by scraping with a hobby knife.

Craft paints work well for painting clothing. A small palette can hold small amounts of several paint colors.

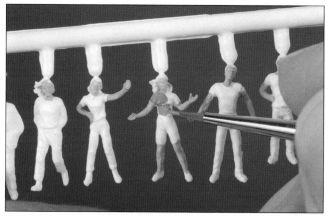

Start by painting light flesh colors and then add progressively darker colors.

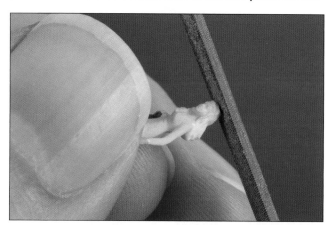

After cutting the figure from its sprue, clean up and shape the head with a needle file.

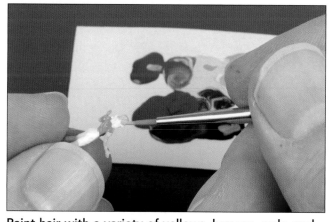

Paint hair with a variety of yellows, browns, reds, and black. Mix the colors for varied effects.

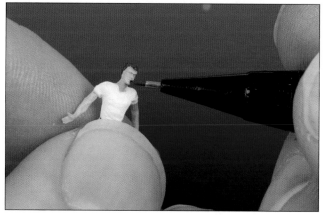

Highlight lips and eyes with a fine-point pencil. Don't try for detail—just add some shadows for realism.

paint—stripes and patterns are difficult to do realistically.

When the body is complete, trim the figure from its sprue and use a needle file to shape the head where it was connected to the sprue.

To paint hair, put several colors on a card scrap, including yellow, black, and various shades of brown and red. Mix the colors with a brush and paint them on. I try to vary the shades on each figure.

In HO and N scales, it's almost impossible to paint mouth or eye features without getting a clown face. Instead, use a fine-point pencil to highlight the lips and eyebrows. From a distance, the light shading that results will look quite realistic.

You can also use these painting techniques to improve or alter commercially painted figures; for example, turning a uniformed guard into a truck driver.

Make sure you place figures in realistic settings and poses. Woodland Scenics Hob-E-Tac is excellent for gluing standing figures, as it remains tacky and allows you to reposition figures if necessary.

Place drivers in vehicles

This Swift truck looks right at home on a city street, with a Preiser driver fully in charge. The truck is an HO model from Classic Metal Works.

A line of model vehicles on a city street can appear very impressive…until someone notices that they're all empty, their scale drivers having apparently abandoned them in the middle of a roadway. Adding drivers to vehicles is not difficult.

All of my examples are in HO scale, but the same techniques apply in other scales as well—although it can be challenging to access the insides of many N scale vehicles.

Start by taking the vehicle apart. It can be as simple as removing a screw or two, or it can involve popping loose some plastic tabs. Some vehicles are glued or riveted together. I would avoid these, as the risk of breaking details or damaging the model is too great.

Most contemporary model vehicles have a basic interior. Often it may be just a seat and a steering wheel. This is usually a solid piece that also serves as a view block so you can't look in a

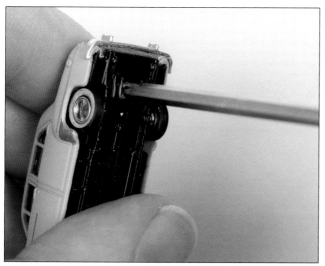

The first step is to get into the vehicle. This Classic Metal Works car has two screws that need to be removed; other models use plastic tabs.

Most figures can be cut down and used in vehicles. Test-fit the figure to ensure that it has adequate headroom.

This CMW truck has a standing, waving Preiser figure that was simply cut off above the waist and glued in position.

This seated Preiser figure had to be trimmed to fit into the Athearn Ford C-series truck cab.

window and see all the way through the floor.

Preiser and other manufacturers offer seated figures, but I've found almost any type of figure can be used. Even seated figures usually have to be trimmed to fit the tight space inside a vehicle, so I often use standing figures and trim them with a hobby knife as needed. Test-fit the figure and then glue it in place with cyanoacrylate adhesive.

Don't worry about where you trim the figure, as once it's installed and the vehicle is back together, you'll only see the upper body through the windshield and windows. It won't be apparent that the figure has no (or only partial) legs.

You can make the figures more visible by removing the glass from the driver-side window. Most models have a single piece of clear plastic molded to the interior. Use a hobby knife to trim away the plastic from the side windows as I did on the pictured Swift and Athearn trucks.

Your vehicles are now ready to hit the roadways.

Open truck doors

The driver swings the trailer doors open prior to making a delivery at a local store in this HO scale scene. Modeling open truck doors and a load adds interest to a scene.

Lots of great vehicle models, especially trucks, are on the market these days. A nice way to create a unique model, as well as a scene, is to open up the vehicle doors and add a visible load. I did this with a 1950s-era Classic Metal Works HO scale semi lettered for Swift's meats, but you can do the same for many other vehicles.

Start by opening the doors. Remove the body from the floor or chassis. Use a razor saw to carefully cut the vertical sides of the doors. Scribing the top seam with a knife allows you to bend and snap the doors free.

The interior needs to be clear. Use a hobby knife to remove any bumps and protrusions on the interior floor. Make a new floor from thin (1/32") sheet wood. Scribe board lines with a hobby knife or just use scribed wood. The floor is just visible at the end, so it only needs to extend 12 scale feet or so inward. I stained the floor with thinned black paint (one part Polly Scale engine black, eight parts distilled water).

I made my trailer load, as explained on pages 8–9, using artwork for a Swift packing crate that I found on the Internet. I reduced the artwork to

Use a razor saw to carefully cut the edges of the door from the body.

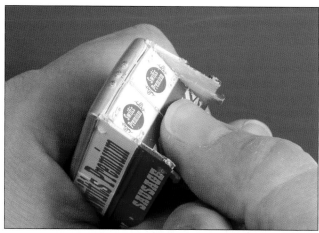

Scribe the top of the doors with a knife until the doors can be flexed and snapped free.

Use a hobby knife with a chisel-tip blade to smooth the semi floor so the new wood floor will sit flush.

Add a new floor of thin sheet or scribed wood, staining it black or dark gray.

The load of crates is a single sheet of graphics that's been cut, folded, and glued in place.

Separate the doors by running a hobby knife down the seam multiple times.

Glue the doors back on the body with CA. It's easiest to fix them in a partially open position.

proper size, printed it on matte photo paper, cut it out, and glued it in place on the trailer floor.

I cut the rear doors apart by scribing repeatedly with a hobby knife, following the latch bar as a guide. Once they were separated, I thinned them by rubbing them against 220 grit sandpaper. Use a

hobby knife and sandpaper to clean up the door openings as needed.

I put small dots of medium cyano-acrylate adhesive (CA) at the hinge moldings and then held each door in place a few seconds until the glue set. I left the doors partially open, so you can still see the lettering. If you model

the doors wide open (swung back completely against the body), you can simply use pieces of .030" styrene painted white or light gray for the doors.

Place the body back on the chassis and your truck is ready to be placed at a loading dock or, as I did, in front of a store ready to make a delivery.

Upgrade a truck

A few simple upgrades in wheels and details greatly improve the appearance of this Atlas HO Ford truck.

Truck models have come a long way in the past few years. Most are based on specific prototype trucks, and many feature a high level of interior and exterior detailing. Many good model trucks, though, can be upgraded with a bit of effort and basic details.

I started with an Atlas HO model of a 1984 Ford LNT semi tractor. The model itself is an accurate model featuring Ford lettering and good body exterior detail, but it is rather plain. Taking the model apart is simple—plastic tabs hold everything together.

Wheels can make a big difference in appearance for trucks. The Atlas model's wheels lacked detail and depth, so I replaced them with a set of Alloy Forms disk wheels (3039). I painted the wheels silver before pressing the tires in place.

The stock model is well rendered and accurate but rather plain.

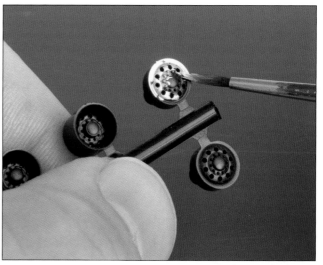

Paint the Alloy Forms wheels silver before pressing the tires into place.

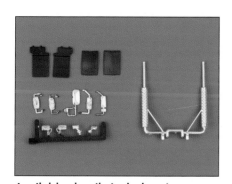

Available details include mirrors and exhaust stacks from Herpa and mud flaps from Lonestar and A-Line.

Adding side mirrors requires drilling mounting holes in the side doors with a pin vise.

A cut-off Preiser figure is glued to the seat. The steering wheel had to be altered, but that is not visible when the model is reassembled.

Wheels on semi tractors are usually chrome; on other trucks, wheels are painted. Check photos (or observe real trucks) for ideas and inspiration. Alloy Forms also offers a set of spoke wheels (3040) perfect for outfitting delivery and other straight trucks with painted wheels.

Other common details that can be added are shown in the lower left photo above. Herpa makes an exhaust stack set (5036) and mirror set (50203), and mud flaps are available from Lonestar (LS12014) and A-Line (50103).

I added mirrors from the Herpa set to the Ford by drilling mounting holes in the side door. Check the fit and then dip the ends of the mirror mounting lugs in cyanoacrylate adhesive and press them in place.

I also added a driver to the cab (as explained on pages 36–37) and license plates (page 44). The horn atop the cab was from my scrapbox, left over from a diesel detail upgrade. I finished the model with door decals for a seed dealer taken from a Microscale decal set, figuring a local truck like this (no sleeper box) would be perfect in service for a feed or seed dealer or a grain elevator.

Check the model trucks in your fleet, and odds are that you can make some of these basic upgrades to many of them.

Detail semitrailers

The Walthers HO trailer at right received a number of detail upgrades including a license plate, builder's plate, and decal lights. I also added an ICC bar and new wheels.

Tractor trailers are frequently found around trains (and industries served by trains), whether they are piggyback trailers or other private or common-carrier trucks. Trailer models are worthy of detailing as much as a boxcar, and dressing them up a bit enhances their look.

Trailer markings are the first thing I look at. Microscale offers a great set of decals for semitrailers in HO (87-852)

and N (60-852). The sheet includes marker lights, license plates, placards, manufacturer logos (for the truck body and mud flaps), and various warning labels.

I added several of these, including lights, license plate, and builder's plate, to a Walthers HO trailer. I did the same to two A-Line Fruehauf Z-Vans.

Equipment upgrades are also available. Wheels are an easy improvement, and A-Line and Lonestar both offer

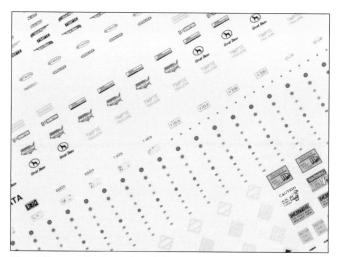

The Microscale 852 decal sheet provides a wealth of details for trailers, including marker lights, warning labels, placards, and builder's insignia.

I added decal marker lights and license plates, mud flaps, and painted hinges and latch bars to this A-Line Fruehauf Z-Van.

Here's another example of an A-Line trailer, lettered with Microscale decals (set 5) and upgraded in similar fashion to the C&NW trailer.

HO scale spoke and disk wheels with separate tires and mud flaps are available from A-Line and Lonestar. Lonestar also offers marker light lenses in several colors.

replacement sets. These two manufacturers also offer mud flaps. Lonestar produces marker and tail lights in red, amber, clear, green, and blue and also makes air suspensions, landing gear, and tire racks.

The Walthers trailer received new wheels, a spare set of Athearn wheels left from another project, which I painted red. It also received an ICC bar—the frame below the back doors that prevents a car from going under

the trailer in a collision. You can easily add one made from scale 4 x 4 styrene strips glued together and painted.

All the trailers received mud flaps. If the model trailer doesn't have a bracket for them, glue a 4 x 4 styrene strip across the underframe behind the wheels and then glue the flaps to the strip.

A bit of paint will also help most factory-painted models. I usually paint everything under the trailer (chassis,

railings, suspension, landing gear) grimy black, unless I know it should be another color. You can add weathering with rust-colored chalk or paint washes if you'd like.

You can also use a fine-point brush to touch up details on the body, including latch bars, latch handles, and hinges.

Your detailed trailers are now ready for placing on streets, highways, loading docks, or piggyback flatcars.

Apply license plates

License plates add a final touch of realism to your vehicles. These are HO cars from Classic Metal Works.

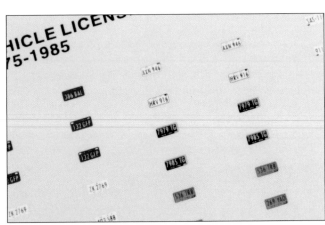

Microscale offers decals for license plates including HO sets MC-4149 and MC-4168.

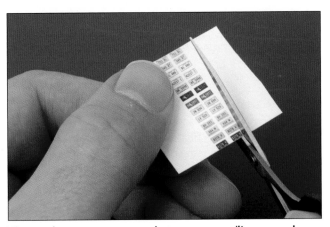

These plates were created at acme.com/licensemaker, sized in Photoshop Elements, and then printed out.

Simply apply decal plates or glue paper license plates in place with a drop of white glue.

License plates are easy to overlook. Few manufacturers add this detail to their models, but adding this detail is simple. Microscale offers two sets of HO decals with a wide variety of plates (MC-4149 and MC-4168 commercial vehicles) and also has sets in N and O scales. If you're modeling a specific location, most vehicles should have the same state plates. This can be a problem since each decal set includes a limited number of plates from each state.

A great option is the website acme. com/licensemaker. You can call up plates from most states from a variety of years and create your own lettering for them. Save the images in photo-editing software, size them, and print them out on matte photo paper. Although this will work in any scale, the lettering is very tough to see in N scale.

North American plates have been standardized at 6 x 12 inches since 1956, with some earlier plates varying in size. All states require back plates, but many states do not require front plates.

Simply apply plate decals or glue paper decals in place with a small dot of white glue or matte medium, and your cars and trucks will be able to legally operate on your scale highways.

Gravel road with grade crossing

These Wisconsin & Southern locomotives lead their train across a timber-framed crossing at a rural gravel road on the HO scale Milwaukee, Racine & Troy.

Glue the wood sections to the ties on either side of each rail. Make sure the tops of the planks are below railhead level, and check the flangeways to make sure they allow free movement of the wheels.

To finish the crossing, add gravel (Highball ballast in this case) between the center timbers and approaching the outside timbers.

Photos by Bill Zuback and Cody Grivno

When updating scenery along a rural stretch of the Kalmbach HO club layout, the Milwaukee, Racine & Troy, I added a stretch of dirt road that crosses the tracks next to some farm fields.

The inspiration for this grade crossing came from *Soo Line Standards: Vol. 3* published by the Soo Line Historical & Technical Society. This plan features a single course of planks on the outside and gauge sides of the rail, with gravel in the middle. Instead of using stripwood, I cut pieces from a Blair Line two-lane, laser-cut wood grade crossing

kit and used sanding sticks to get the wood to the correct thickness.

I attached the wood crossing planks to the plastic ties with cyanoacrylate adhesive, using accelerator to make the bond almost instantaneous. Then I stained the planks with an India ink wash (2 teaspoons ink to 1 pint of 70 percent isopropyl alcohol).

The dirt road was made with Highball Products N scale limestone ballast, so at the crossing, I used this material to fill the gap between the planks on the gauge side of the rail. To prevent the ballast from drying solid on the surface and remaining loose below, I

applied it in two layers. First, I brushed some diluted white glue between the planks and then sprinkled on some ballast. Once this dried, I vacuumed up the excess ballast and applied a second layer. I used a pipette to soak the second layer of ballast with 70 percent isopropyl alcohol and then applied Woodland Scenics Scenic Cement with a pipette. I did the same in building up the road leading to the crossing.

That's all there is to it. To finish the scene, add a set of crossbucks (available from JL Innovative Design, Rix, Tichy, and others).

—Cody Grivno

Asphalt road with grade crossing

Photos by David Popp

A FedEx van rolls to a stop at a grade crossing on the HO scale Wisconsin & Southern, a project layout built by the *Model Railroader* staff.

Model Railroader's HO scale Wisconsin & Southern project railroad needed two grade crossings. There are several easy-to-install grade crossing kits from Blair Line, BLMA, Walthers, and others, so I selected a Blair Line 165 wood grade crossing and got to work. These have laser-cut grooves to simulate individual planks.

I glued the wood piece between the rails with cyanoacrylate adhesive (CA). Before cementing the approach planks on the outside of the rails, I sanded the backs of the wood parts with 220 grit sandpaper, so they wouldn't sit above the tops of the rail.

Once everything had a day to dry, I painted the surrounding ground and the roadway shoulders with flat tan latex paint. Next, I stained the wood crossing. I made my own stain by putting a few drops of isopropyl alcohol in a paint jar cap. I mixed the alcohol with one brush full of Polly Scale UP Dark Gray and then brushed it on the wood grade crossing. The stain settled into the plank and spike recesses, making the details stand out.

Stain the Blair Line parts with a thinned mix of dark gray paint. Paint the edges of the styrene roadway base with flat tan latex paint.

Press the Busch road material in place as you gradually remove the protective backing material.

A set of Tomar crossing signals, plus an instrument cabinet and battery box, finish the scene.

Pavement markings are easy to add using an airbrush and etched-brass template from S&S Hobby Products.

After the scenery paint was dry, I applied the road material. I used Busch self-adhesive roadway. This thin foam material is 3⅛" wide, comes with or without printed pavement markings, and may be laid straight or in gentle curves. It's very easy to work with, and I like its realistic asphalt appearance.

With its backing still on, I set the Busch road on top of the styrene and cork roadway base to measure its length. I then cut the pieces I needed with a pair of scissors. To apply the road, I started at the grade crossing and worked my way out. Since the road material is very flexible, starting at the crossing helped maintain an even edge where the road meets the wood approach planks.

I peeled the backing off as I pressed the foam to the styrene. (Avoid the temptation to peel the backing off all at once!) This technique makes the material much easier to handle and keeps wrinkles and stretching to a minimum.

With the road applied, I added Highball Products N Scale Limestone Ballast to the shoulders. (For N scale roads, I use silica sand, which is finer.) I installed the shoulders by painting a ⅜" strip of white glue (diluted 10 percent with water) along the edge of the road and sifted the ballast into the glue with a spoon. I vacuumed up the excess ballast from the road surface before applying Woodland Scenics Scenic Cement to the shoulders. Be careful not to use too much: Scenic Cement can soak into the foam road surface and discolor it. Any surrounding scenery can also be finished.

I installed a pair of Tomar Industries H-862 crossing signals. These detailed, assembled models can be wired to operate with the addition of a flasher circuit. I drilled ⅛" holes in the scenery, fed the wires through the holes, and set the signals in place on their brass mounting posts. Friction holds them in place.

Real crossing signals have an instrument cabinet and battery box nearby. I found metal castings in our scrapbox for the cabinet and battery vault. For similar results, you can use a Details West 902 cabinet and 910 battery box. After painting the castings in appropriate colors, I secured them with white glue.

I added pavement markings to the grade crossing approaches. (If you're modeling an earlier era, skip this step.) I used my airbrush and an etched brass template from S&S Hobby Products.

I positioned the template on the roadway, masked the surrounding area with tape, and sprayed the pavement with a light coat of Polly Scale reefer white. To make the stop lines in front of the signals, I masked off all of the template except a single line. I then used the single line template to airbrush the stop lines for both signals, which completed the grade crossings.

—*David Popp*

Paint and detail track

The streaked, rusty appearance of this Walthers HO flextrack makes it look much more like real track. The rail joint bars are a nice detail touch as well.

Painted track greatly improves a layout's appearance. Without some help, commercial flex and sectional track just don't look right, with shiny nickel-silver rails and molded brown or black plastic ties. Adding paint and rail joint bars are simple steps to improve it.

The best time to detail and paint track is after it's in place but before ballast is applied. You can paint track before laying it, but bending flextrack can slide the plastic spikes and expose spots of unpainted rail. You can also paint track that's already been ballasted—it just

takes a bit more care to avoid getting stray paint on ballast and scenery.

Joint bars are a nice detail that takes track to a new level. Real track (except for welded rail) has a joint every 39 feet (the most common length of rail through the late 1900s). I used the Details West cast-metal HO versions on Walthers flextrack (921 with six bolts, 922 with four bolts). They're also available from proto87.com in HO and N scales.

To add joint bars, use a toothpick to add a drop of cyanoacrylate adhesive (CA) at the proper place on the web

To add a joint bar, place a drop of medium viscosity CA on the rail web at the proper location.

Place the joint bar in position and hold it for a couple of seconds until the glue sets.

Floquil's enamel paint markers work well for painting rail. Layer multiple rust colors to get a varied effect.

Painting ties kills their plastic shine, making them much more realistic. Use a mix of brown, gray, and black paint.

of the rail and then add the joint bar. Place one on each side of the rail. Joints are usually staggered so they aren't directly opposite each other. Make sure that joint bars on the inside of the rail don't interfere with wheel flanges.

Adding joint bars to an entire layout can be a daunting project, so many modelers just use them in foreground scenes where they'll be more visible.

Paint the rails a dark rust color. Rail color is rarely uniform, so use several colors. You can use a brush to paint them Polly Scale Rail Brown (414416) and Railroad Tie Brown

(414329), mixing in some grimy black and black on occasion. A handy alternative is Floquil's line of enamel paint markers. The company's track color set includes rail brown, railroad tie brown, and rust.

Paint each side of each rail with a rust color. It's good to also coat the spikes and tie plates as well. Follow this with a second coat of another rust color. (I suggest starting with light rust colors and following with darker colors.) The result will be a streaked, varied look. As soon as the paint dries, use an abrasive track cleaner (such as a

Walthers Bright Boy) to clean the tops of the rails.

Next, paint the ties. New wood ties are usually dark brown to dark gray (almost black) in color, and as they age, they turn lighter gray or brown. I place a few drops of black, grimy black, dark brown, and rust in a small lid and brush-paint ties with various mixes of these colors.

Concrete ties (found on many main lines with welded rail) are a uniform light gray color. They can be brush-painted or airbrushed, and then the rails can be painted as described earlier.

Build an operating derail

Photos by Matt Snell

A hinged derail and folding marker sign protect the main line on Matt Snell's HO scale layout. If the boxcar rolls, the derail will stop it before it fouls the main track.

To keep cars on sidings and spurs from accidentally rolling onto a main track, prototype railroads use a device called a *derail*. Derails shove a renegade car's wheels off the rail and stop it from moving farther. On industrial sidings that border mainline tracks or on tracks where unloading equipment has been attached to a car, hinged, manually operated derails are common protection.

One popular design consists of two main pieces: a base that's mounted to the ties and a derailing block that's placed on the rail, connected by a heavy-duty hinge. When in the derailing position, the block rests on the railhead; in the non-derailing position, it's out of the way between the rails.

Derails are generally painted in bright colors and marked with signs mounted beside the track (common in older eras) or on a staff attached to the derail that folds down when the derail is off.

While searching for a solution to creeping cars on my HO layout, I found a derail casting (Sequoia Scale Models 2006). [This derail, and similar

This prototype hinged derail is double-ended and will derail cars from either direction.

This HO derail is a two-piece, white-metal casting.

To convert the white-metal casting to a working model, drill two holes in the base for the hinge.

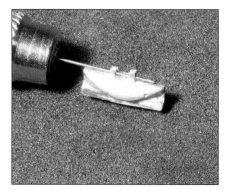

Drill a hole for the hinge through the "fingers" of the derailing block. The block will turn on a wire threaded through the holes.

Looping a wire through the holes and bending the ends down forms the hinge on which the derailing block will pivot.

To make the installation more secure, glue the ends of the wire into holes drilled into the track and roadbed.

products, can be found online through walthers.com, debenllc.com, and other sites.] The white-metal casting matches a prototype double-end, hinged-block derail. When installed on the track, it will either act as a true derail or simply block cars from rolling.

To make this two-piece casting a working model, begin by test-fitting the base onto a piece of track and inserting the flange on the bottom of the casting between the ties. If the flange interferes with the placement on the ties, remove the flange with a chisel blade or jeweler's file so the casting will sit flush on the ties.

To make the derail operable, it needs to be hinged so it can be opened and closed. Drill two no. 78 holes through the base casting, one at each of the corners that form an L angle close to the rail. Next, drill two holes through the fingers that extend from the top casting, locating these holes as close to the body of the casting as possible. The excess length of the fingers can be removed

with flush cutters or a file to ensure that the derail won't hang up on the ballast when operated.

Insert a length of .015" brass wire through the holes in the top casting and bend each end 90 degrees to form a U shape. This wire can then be inserted through the holes in the base casting to form a hinge.

Before trimming off the excess wire, place the derail assembly onto a piece of scrap track and adjust the height of the derail block so it seats properly on the rail. Trim away the excess wire with wire cutters. Apply a drop of cyanoacrylate adhesive (CA) to the underside of the base to secure the wire in place. If you'd like to strengthen the assembly, leave the wire long and drill holes for it into the roadbed. Use CA to cement the excess wire into these holes.

For older eras, a post-mounted sign can be placed next to the derail using a sign kit or decals applied to a styrene background. Modern-era modelers can add a simple fold-down

sign on the ties adjacent to the derail. I used an N.J. International fold-down sign (part of the 1308 blue safety sign set), removing its stick-on lettering and relettering it for a derail with a white decal alphabet.

The derail should be placed in a location that will stop the wheels of the longest car without allowing the body to extend past the siding's clearance point. Since the derail is manually operated, it should be within easy reach. Make sure buildings or trees are not in your way.

Test the derail to ensure ample clearance for low-hanging items such as locomotive pilots and plows. After making any necessary adjustments, secure the base with CA and paint it yellow.

To open the derail, flip the hinged block backward off the rail. To apply it, flip the block onto the rail. You should then not have to worry about any cars fouling your main track again.

—*Matt Snell*

Detail a signal

Photo by Bruce Petty

On Bruce Petty's HO Los Angeles & San Fernando Valley layout, hanging code line cable completes the signal detailing. The cable, strung between the pole box and signal box, is made from .035" styrene rod and .003" copper wire.

Whether you have working or nonworking lineside signals on your layout, you can add a few additional details to improve their realism. I chose to model a realistic signal system on my HO scale Los Angeles & San Fernando Valley Railroad as much for accuracy as for practicality. Signal wiring is a great way to add visual interest in a small space.

On prototype railroads, the wires that run pole to pole along rights-of-way carry electrical impulses that operate signals and control the movement of

trains. At the beginning of each siding are signals and instrument cases that house relays and other electrical signal equipment. The wires connect at a pole box just under the crossarm, forming the heavy code line cable that runs to the instrument case. Because the heavy cable can't support itself between any two points, it must be slung under a messenger cable and held in place with clips.

I found modeling this detail to be quite simple. I was able to model the cable's hanging look on my layout using some styrene rods, copper lamp cord wire, and Testor's grimy black paint.

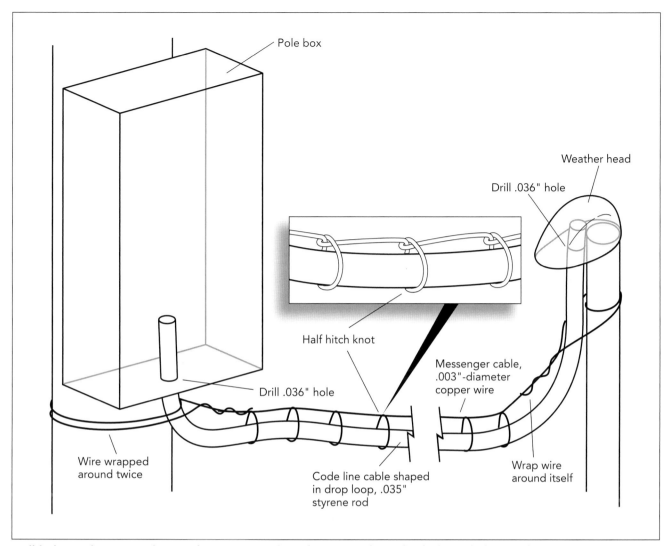

Labels in illustration:
- Pole box
- Weather head
- Drill .036" hole
- Half hitch knot
- Messenger cable, .003"-diameter copper wire
- Drill .036" hole
- Wire wrapped around twice
- Code line cable shaped in drop loop, .035" styrene rod
- Wrap wire around itself

Drill holes with a no. 64 bit, so the styrene rod can be inserted into both the pole box and the weather head. Wrap the extra copper wire around the pole and weather head to keep the rod in place. *Illustration by Jay Smith*

I started by making the pole box. Southern Pacific pole boxes measured 6" x 18" x 24" and had a wood frame cased by sheet tin with doors on the front. I cut strip styrene (Evergreen .080" x .250") to length to make the box and painted it silver to match the prototype.

I then drilled no. 64 holes (.036") in the instrument case, the signal mast, and the bottom of the pole box, where the cable would be attached.

I modeled the cable using Evergreen Scale Models styrene .035" rod (220) and a copper wire strand for the messenger cable. The .003"-diameter copper strand can be found in common lamp cord wire.

First, I curved the styrene into a drop loop to replicate the hanging look of the heavy code line wire bundle.

After softening the styrene with a little heat from a hair dryer, I bent it around a ⅛" drill bit to help form the drop loop. Drop loops can vary in curvature depending on the prototype, so the loop doesn't have to be perfect. I shaped the styrene with the shank of the bit, bending the rod while moving along its length.

To make the clips that connect the code line cable to the messenger cable, I made a series of half hitch knots in the copper wire starting at the beginning of the drop loop. I spaced the knots a scale 8" to 12" apart, pulling each snug. It's important to leave about 1" of extra wire beyond the drop loop on both ends to use as tie-offs to the signal case and to the pole box.

Once I had made the final copper wire knots at the ends of the drop loop,

I cut the styrene rod after the bend. I then made sure the rod would fit into the bottom hole of the pole box and used the extra inch of copper wire to tie around the pole. The extra wire is also handy for holding the finished code line cable while painting the rod and wire grimy black.

After test-fitting the styrene rod and making any necessary adjustments, I used cyanoacrylate adhesive to glue the ends into the pole box and relay case holes. I then looped the copper wire ends around the pole and weather head connections and tied off both sides by wrapping the remaining wire around itself. With the wire and styrene in place, I made a few last paint touch-ups with the grimy black.

—Bruce Petty

Signs along the tracks

Among the most common sign types are mileposts, left, and whistle posts, center. This is an HO set of Stewart F units painted in Chicago Great Western colors.

Drive along railroad tracks for even a mile or two and you'll notice a wide variety of signs along the right-of-way. Placing replicas of these signs along your model right-of-way greatly improves realism.

When looking for signs, sets offered by Blair Line, JL Innovative Design, and other companies are a good source. The Blair Line sheet shown in the photo on the opposite page (HO 101) is also available in N and O scales.

Using the signs is easy—just cut them from the sheet with a sharp hobby knife, using a straightedge as a guide, or with a small scissors. Then use a small dab of white glue to fix them to a signpost. Blair Line includes lengths of stripwood in its kits that you can stain or paint black, dark gray, or brown to represent wood posts. You can also make your own posts from scale 4 x 4 or 6 x 6 scale stripwood.

To simulate steel posts, use lengths of styrene rod or wire painted black or dark gray.

You can also make your own signs. Many railroads had unique styles for

Manufacturers such as Blair Line offer sheets of right-of-way signs on thin plastic or paper. Use a hobby knife or small scissors to cut them out.

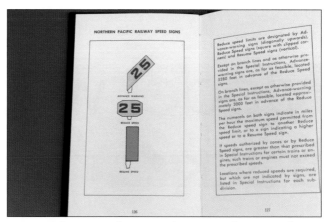

You can also scan photos or drawings of signs and print them out. These illustrations are from a book of operating rules from the 1960s.

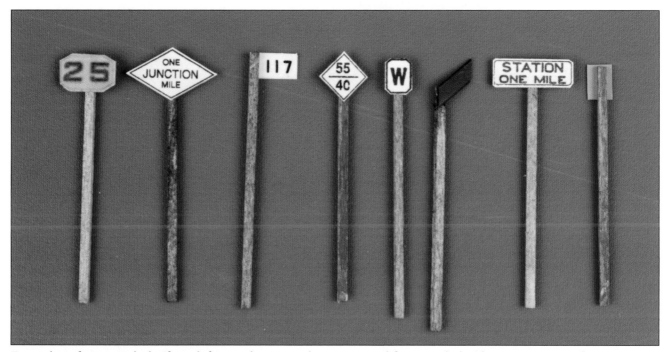

Examples of signs include (from left) a reduce speed sign scanned from a rule book, junction sign (Blair Line), milepost (dry transfer on thin white styrene), speed sign (Blair Line), whistle post (Blair Line), flanger lift sign (styrene painted black), station one mile (N Scale Architect), and the back of a whistle post.

their whistle posts, mile markers, and speed signs. If you can take a photo (or find a photo on the Internet), you can scale it to proper size and print it out. I did this with the speed signs shown in the photo, which I found in a late-1960s edition of the *Consolidated Code of Operating Rules*.

In the photo above, you can see a collection of different signs. The most common are whistle posts and flanger warning signs. Whistle posts come in many designs, with the most common being a black W on a white square. They are placed in advance of grade

crossings to signal the engineer to blow the proper whistle or horn signal (two longs, a short, and a long).

Flanger signs (usually a plain black board at an angle) are also located ahead of crossings. They tell snow-plow operators to lift the flanger (part of the plow blade that extends down between the rails) so it won't damage the crossing.

Speed signs indicate limits for freight and passenger trains, and speed restriction signs list limits on curves, bridges, and other areas where trains must slow down.

Mileposts are located at every mile on real railroads. These are often on their own posts, or they can be placed on neighboring communication poles. Placing them according to prototype practice is limiting (one every 60 feet in HO scale), so many modelers fudge a bit and locate them every 10 feet or so.

Other signs provide clearance information; mark yard limits; and warn of approaching junctions, stations, and yards. Keep your eyes open for chances to add signs and also check photos and the prototype itself for examples.

Model weed-grown track

An overgrown, weedy stretch of track makes for a more-believable industrial spur than does one with finely manicured ballast.

Not all actual track features carefully maintained ballast. Especially along industrial spurs and seldom-used lines, you'll find weedy track with just the rails poking out. Modeling a stretch of this track helps capture the authenticity of that location.

I suggest finishing the surrounding scenery first. For this example, I added an industrial spur on a section of an HO diorama that was already scenicked, and the techniques are the same regardless of scale. You can also do this directly on top of track that's already been ballasted.

Start by mixing ballast with fine ground foam. Many spurs, sidings, and branch lines, especially in the steam era, had cinder ballast. To capture this look, I mixed Woodland Scenics fine cinders ballast with green blend fine ground foam. Note that the track is already painted.

Sprinkle the mix over the track as you would with ordinary ballast. However, when spreading it with a soft brush, don't be afraid to completely

Mix ballast with fine ground foam and spread it between the rails and along them as well.

Use a soft brush to spread the material, covering some of the ties completely.

Soak the foam/ballast mix with rubbing alcohol applied with a pipette or eyedropper.

Saturate the track with diluted white glue. An old saline-solution bottle makes for a handy applicator.

The bumper is made of two pieces of stripwood, stained and cut at angles, and then planted in the ballast mix.

cover the ties in some places. Add more ground foam as needed to get the appearance you're looking for. Keep the inside of each railhead clear so that wheels can roll freely.

Soak the ballasted area with 70 percent rubbing alcohol to allow the glue to penetrate the material. Applying it with a pipette provides a great deal of control. You can also use water with a few drops of dish detergent added, but I prefer using alcohol. It doesn't disturb the scenery material as much as water does, and it evaporates quicker.

Add a mix of one part white glue and four parts water to the area. I use an old contact-lens container as a dispenser; you can use an eyedropper or pipette as well.

I added the railroad-tie bumper shown before gluing the ballast. The ties are lengths of stripwood cut at an angle to make them look like they're deeply buried. Press them in place before gluing the ballast.

Once the glue dries, clean the rails and run a car along the track. Remove any stray ballast or scenery

material that rubs the wheels. You can further detail the track by gluing bits of coarse or extra-coarse ground foam in place, or by adding weeds or grass tufts (see pages 60–61 for some ideas)—just make sure that the materials don't get in the way of operations.

You can also use this technique to model passing sidings, branch lines, and secondary lines, varying the amount of grass and weeds to suit. Look at photos and real railroads and let prototype examples be your guide.

Add junk between yard tracks

A wide array of cast-off garbage and spills surround yard tracks on Bill Aldrich's HO layout.

Photo by Paul Dolkos

When weathering a freight yard, adding some junk and garbage along the tracks can give your right-of-way a more detailed appearance. Just be judicious in locating these details. Junk wouldn't be found along busy yard tracks, where the materials would be a significant hazard to on-ground yard workers. It would most likely be found along a clean-out track, where it would probably be taken care of rather quickly, or perhaps along a seldom-used siding or spur track.

The photo of Bill Aldrich's layout shows paper trash and other types of junk. Paper trash can include posters, newspapers, and brown paper scraps that simulate packing materials.

You can scan actual newspaper pages, reduce them to the proper scale with a computer, and print them out. Cut the papers to size, add some creases, and scatter them about.

For discarded shipping materials, paint wire to represent strapping and break or cut lengths of stripwood for pallet pieces and other wood scraps.

Broken glass can be simulated by cutting pieces of .005"-thick clear styrene. The spilled material around the split-open sack can be made from colored chalk or ground foam. Between the rails, you can also add small amounts of cargo, such as grain or coal, that leaked from hoppers.

Small oil drips from railcar bearings can be painted on the ties and ballast between the rails. You can also add a variety of vegetation between and around yard tracks to complete the scene.

—Paul Dolkos

Use forced perspective

The HO scale church looked too close to the tracks, which ruined the desired effect of having a steeple poking above distant treetops.

Substituting an N scale model provided the solution and made the church look like a more-distant structure. *Photos by Marty McGuirk*

Forced perspective is one of the best techniques for turning inches into miles. Forced perspective is not the same as selective compression, where the goal is reducing the size of a prototype structure without losing key identifying elements (for example, modeling a grain elevator with 6 silos instead of the prototype's 12).

The key difference is the scale of the finished model. Forced perspective means building a model to a smaller scale to make it appear farther away. For layouts, this usually means adding background buildings built to a smaller scale than the rest of the layout.

Initially, I planned to build an HO scale model of a New England church for one scene on my layout. I wanted

the scene to look complete but hadn't selected a prototype church to model, so as a filler, I purchased an HO scale cutout paper New England village published by Dover, which included a church that I assembled and placed in the scene.

Although it was located some distance from the tracks, the church appeared too close. I wanted the steeple poking through the treetops in the distance. The solution was to obtain another Dover building, this time reducing it on a color photocopier to N scale (54 percent reduction). I used spray adhesive to bond the paper walls to .015" styrene, which produced a sturdy model.

Placing the N scale church in the scene immediately conveyed the sense

of distance. Surrounding the church with trees blended it into the scene and made the trickery less obvious.

I also used forced perspective to add a small village green and a road in front of the church. It's unconvincing to take foreground elements, like roads, directly to the backdrop, so instead I ran the road behind some trees and a low hill, having it reemerge, reduced in width, "in the distance."

Avoid placing models of different scales next to each other. The obvious size differences between the two can easily give the trick away. Keep the larger, full scale structures in the foreground with the forced perspective buildings in the background.

—*Marty McGuirk*

Weeds from fake fur

Photos by Sergio Slonecki

Clumps of fake-fur weeds enhance the desert scene on Sergio Slonecki's southwestern-themed HO scale layout.

Weeds and tall grasses are among the most common sights in nature. I have an HO scale layout that represents southwestern California, and weeds and grass tufts are everywhere. To represent these plants, you can use Silflor prairie tufts, which are ready-to-place grass clusters, or you can create your own following my technique. I use fake fur to create realistic grass tufts.

Fake fur is available in many colors and can be found in fabric stores. I was lucky enough to find a natural tan color similar to what is seen in the desert. If you can't find a color that matches the scenery on your layout, you can dye the fur to your liking. It's not as easy as dying cotton fabric, but you can do it using textile dyes. I recommend trying to find an olive green or light brown dye. You can make different shades of color by using different amounts of dye.

I bought a paraffin wax block at an arts and crafts store and drilled a ³⁄₁₆"-deep hole into the block using a ⅛" bit. The hole is used to form the "root" of the grass tuft.

Fake fur is available in several different colors, making it easier to match the region and season you're modeling.

After making several weed tufts, plant them on the layout in ⅛" holes drilled into the scenery. Then use white glue to secure the tufts.

Add detail to the weeds by lightly brushing some of them with acrylic paint.

To make a grass tuft, cut a small portion of fake fur from the backing and twist one end between your fingers. Place three to four drops of cyanoacrylate adhesive (CA) into the hole in the wax block and quickly insert the twisted end of the fur into the adhesive. CA bonds quickly, so I use gloves to make sure it doesn't get on my hands.

Hold the fur in the CA for a few seconds and then remove it. Don't leave the fibers in the CA for too long or the tuft will adhere to the wax block.

After pulling the tuft out of the hole, apply a drop of CA accelerator to the base to set the adhesive and then lay the tuft aside and make another one. After making several grass tufts, use scissors to trim them as needed.

To plant the weed tufts, I drill ⅛" holes in the scenery, place a drop of white glue into each hole, and insert the grass tufts.

I've found that creating clusters of weeds using different colors produces the best results. I also add touches of

detail to the grasses using various colors of acrylic paint applied with a soft brush. In the photos, you can see the subtle differences between the weeds.

This technique also works well for making small bushes. When doing so, add some ground foam to the tufts to represent leaves. To enhance a landscape even more, cover the area with static grass before planting the tufts. The end result looks natural and realistic.

—*Sergio Slonecki*

Make realistic trees

Photos by Marty McGuirk

Modeling a forest of good-looking trees, such as these on Marty McGuirk's HO layout, is easy using SuperTrees.

The pursuit of perfect model trees is something of a hobby within the hobby for some model railroaders. But for the rest of us, especially those who don't model the desert, trees are a necessary evil. We need them for our railroads to look plausible—the problem is that we need lots of them.

Many methods of making trees have been developed over the years. Some of the best-looking trees I've come across are SuperTrees from Scenic Express. I like their realistic look, the easy way you can model trees that

have lost some or all their leaves, and the speed with which you can forest a large area.

Out of the package, the trees hardly look realistic. To give the trees and branches the proper color, I spray them flat dark gray. Any cheap dark gray primer will work—just make sure the paint is flat, not glossy.

Then soak the tree armatures in a pan or tray of diluted matte medium (one part matte medium to five parts water) for several minutes. Dipping them won't do. You need to make sure the material soaks in the mix.

After spraying the tree material (at left) with flat dark gray paint, it begins to look like a real tree, as shown at right.

Soak the armatures in diluted matte medium for several minutes to seal them.

Sprinkle fine ground foam on the armatures while the matte medium is still wet.

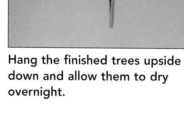

Hang the finished trees upside down and allow them to dry overnight.

If you are tempted to use hair spray instead of matte medium as an adhesive—don't. The matte medium seals and preserves the armature. If you use hair spray to secure the foliage in place, the trees will eventually crumble to dust.

Sprinkle fine ground foam onto the still-wet matte medium. For best results, hold the tree upright using a set of tweezers and sprinkle the foam from above. Use various greens for spring and summer trees. I model fall scenery, but find most fall color ground foams to be too garish. I use Scenic Express' line of fine fall ground foam colors. These are available in a wide range of shades and textures that are subdued enough to create a realistic fall landscape.

To straighten the trunk, clip a weight, such as a clothespin or tweezers, to the top of the tree. Hang the trees upside down and allow them to dry overnight. Once they dry, they're ready for planting in scenery.

—*Marty McGuirk*

Plant a soybean field

An HO scale Chicago Great Western train rolls past a soybean field in a typical Midwestern scene.

If you model rural farmland, you'll need to have farm fields and pastures. Some crops can be difficult to model, but it is relatively easy to add a decent representation of a soybean field to an HO scale scene. Soybean fields can be found throughout the Midwest, farther south along the Mississippi River, and in many areas along the East Coast.

I started by making a plowed field (which can be a good scene in itself).

The field can be level or situated on rolling hills. Start by painting an area with flat black or dark gray latex paint. (The color should be close to that of the dirt you're using.)

I used real dirt for my field, taken from my backyard and sifted through a window screen to get rid of rocks and large chunks. Sprinkle the dirt on the wet paint and then form the furrows. I did this by dragging the dirt with a comb that I had modified by removing

You can use a comb with some teeth removed to form parallel furrows in the dirt.

Apply Scenic Cement along the furrows. You don't need to follow the furrows precisely for an effective look.

Press coarse ground foam in place over the glue. Work in small areas so the glue doesn't soak in too quickly.

Once the glue dries, vacuum up stray foam. After vacuuming, you are left with rows of green plants.

teeth in an even pattern. The appearance doesn't have to be perfect. You just want the look of parallel furrows in the dirt.

Once it looks good, soak the dirt with rubbing alcohol and apply diluted white glue to secure it. (Follow the same directions as adhering the ground foam mix on pages 56–57). Then let the field dry.

The soybean plants are represented by Woodland Scenics coarse green

ground foam. Apply Woodland Scenics Scenic Cement along the furrows. Work in a small area—no more than 3" x 6" at a time. Before the cement begins to soak in, add ground foam on top of it and press it into place. Keep working in small areas until the field is complete. Again, the rows don't have to be perfect—you're just aiming for the appearance of plants in separate rows.

Let the glue dry overnight. Vacuum up the ground foam that didn't stick.

(You can also salvage much of it for reuse by simply scooping it up by hand and then vacuuming the rest). You can fine-tune the field's appearance by picking foam from where it shouldn't be and then adding more glue and ground foam where it is needed.

This will give your model farmers a thriving crop they can take to the local elevator when harvest time rolls around in fall.

Add cattails to a water scene

Photos by Lee Vande Visse

Adding cattails and a dead tree greatly improve the detailing around this swamp scene on Lee Vande Visse's O scale narrow gauge layout.

I wanted to add some cattails to a water scene on my On3 narrow gauge layout. You can adjust my techniques a bit to get the same effects in HO scale.

Cattails are common pond plants, and I added them before pouring the casting-resin water in my swamp. You can also add them to scenes that are already completed.

I make the cattails by adding dense brown flower pods to thin stalks made of wire or dried weeds. I used stalks a bit longer than needed, so I could trim them to size during installation.

Paper strips roughly scale 6" to 8" high and 2 or 3 scale feet long work as flower pods. I soaked the paper in a bath of thinned white glue (one part glue to five parts water) until the paper's stiffness disappeared.

I placed one strip on my index finger, set a stalk in position, and rolled the end together with my thumb. The paper dries slowly, so you can make adjustments until the pod's shape looks right. This technique takes some practice, but once you master it, you can quickly turn out the cattails. Let the finished cattails dry overnight and then you can paint them.

A small foam block is handy for holding the cattails during drying and painting.

The cattail leaves come from dried flower material from a craft shop.

Pour the water material into the pond or swamp area. EnviroTex and other water materials will level themselves before drying.

The Campbell cast-metal tree trunk has holes that allow you to easily add branches. Give the completed tree a coat of light gray paint to finish weathering it.

I used Polly Scale buff on the dry stalks and roof brown on the flower pods.

The long, sword-like leaves of my cattail plants came from the dried flower section of a craft shop. I sprayed them with several coats of clear flat spray paint to keep them from deteriorating. I then glued the leaves together in small bunches.

Once the leaves were in place and the white glue had dried, I added the cattails. I trimmed each one to a pleasing height and inserted it in the middle of the leaves with a small drop of white glue. Cattails bunched in groups of three or four look more natural than individual plants.

Dead trees and a few tree stumps add to the realism of a pond. My pine tree armatures, appropriate to the Rocky Mountains, are from Campbell Scale Models. The pine tree trunks come stained dark brown and contain dozens of small holes for branches.

To make working on the tree easier, I placed the trunk in a hole drilled in a block of wood that served as a handle. Then I added a few twigs from the dried flowers I used in the cattails—they're perfect for dead, broken branches. You can also use small twigs from your yard. To attach, apply a small drop of cyanoacrylate adhesive

(CA) to the branch, slip it into the hole in the trunk, and spray the joint with CA accelerator. If small blotches of white appear from excess CA, you can touch up these areas with a brush and brown paint.

Airbrush the finished trees with light gray paint to dull the color a bit and make the dead trees look more weathered.

I plant my trees by drilling a hole slightly smaller than the trunk and then tapering the trunk until it fits tightly. Cover the base with a few pinches of peat moss or ground foam secured with diluted white glue.

—*Lee Vande Visse*

Build and install board fences

This HO Central Valley board fence keeps people from straying from the sidewalk to the neighboring rail spur.

Board fences are great details to add to a scene. They can serve as view blocks, help separate scenes, and provide security around your scale industries and businesses.

I built a pair of these fences for a city scene: one to run along a sidewalk to keep people off the neighboring railroad track, and the other to keep

my scale figures away from a vacant lot next to a brick structure.

Central Valley makes an injection-molded styrene HO fence (1601) that's almost ready to use, with grain detail molded in place. This kit also includes three other styles of fencing as well.

I brush-painted the fence with Polly Scale reefer white. I only gave the fence one coat of paint, letting some of the

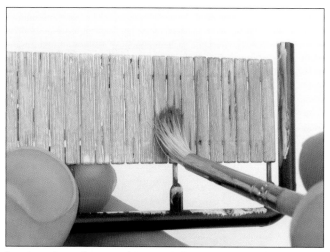

I painted my fence white and then weathered it with dark gray chalk applied with a stiff brush.

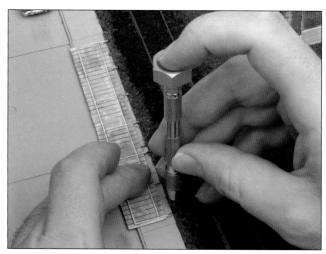

Use the fence as a guide for drilling mounting holes in the scenery base.

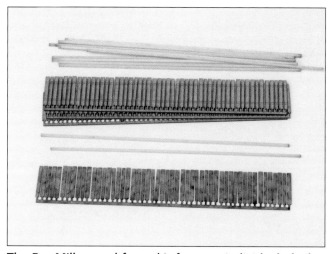

The Bar Mills wood fence kit features individual planks, held together temporarily by a fret, with separate strips for runners and posts.

The completed Bar Mills fence captures the look of unpainted wood.

original dark gray color show through. This gives the look of a fence that had been in the weather for awhile. I also brushed on some dark gray chalk.

Planting the fence was a matter of drilling holes for the molded posts. Use the fence itself as a guide for drilling mounting holes. A bit of cyanoacrylate adhesive (CA) on each post holds it in place.

I wanted a fence in reasonably good repair, but if you want a more run-down look you can cut out individual boards, or vary the fence by cutting down the height of some planks.

To model a bare wood fence, nothing beats the look of real wood. For my second fence, I used a Bar Mills laser-cut wood Insta-Fence kit (42), which is also available in N scale (41).

The kit is easy to assemble. I used white glue to secure the stringers to the back of the fence and then glued the posts in place per the instructions. I weathered this fence with some dark gray chalk and glued the posts in place behind the sidewalk next to a building. You could also stain or paint the fence, but be sure to coat both sides to minimize warping of the wood parts.

Rural wire fences

A group of HO scale cows watch behind a typical wire fence as a Burlington Route passenger train rolls past.

If you have a stretch of right-of-way or highway running through a rural area, consider adding a wire fence. These fences are everywhere in rural areas, especially in the farm and ranch lands of the Midwest, West, and Plains states.

Modeling this type of fence is an easy project, although you'll need a lot of fence posts. While scale 6 x 6 strip-wood works well for HO scale posts, I like to use square wood toothpicks. Each can be cut in half with a razor

saw, yielding two posts with pointed ends that allow for easy planting. The toothpicks also have the rough-cut look of real fence posts.

I stain the posts with a thinned mix of grimy black, black, or rail brown paint. Mix one part paint with about six parts water, and brush the various colors on the posts. You can use a piece of foam insulation to hold posts while painting.

Plant the posts in the ground in a straight line or to follow the curve

Stain fence posts with a thinned mix of black and brown paint.

Poke or drill holes in the scenery. Then put a touch of glue at the bottom of each post and push it in place.

Add a drop of CA to the post and hold the EZ Line in place with tweezers until the glue sets.

of the tracks or a highway. For foam scenery, simply push the posts in place. You'll need to drill holes in other types of scenery. Posts should have consistent spacing. Typical post spacing is 16 feet; this can be tighter for crowded pastures or in high-wind areas, or broader (to 25 feet) for pastures holding fewer cattle. Add a touch of glue to the bottom of each post before pushing it in place. Each post should stand about 50 scale inches out of the ground.

For wire, I prefer EZ Line from Berkshire Junction. This elastic thread works beautifully to simulate wires of many types, as it won't sag once applied (as common thread can do), and it will stretch and return to shape if bumped. Available in fine and heavy sizes, it comes in black, gray, rust, and other colors. Either fine rust or gray is good for fences. I used rust for this project.

Three to five strands are common on real fences, but I find that two wires are enough to provide a realistic

impression. Use a toothpick to apply a bit of cyanoacrylate adhesive (CA) to a post. Pull the EZ Line taut and use a tweezers to hold it to the post a few seconds until it sets. Repeat until all the wire is installed.

You can get fancy and install extra bracing posts at the corners if you'd like, and you can find many examples online of how this is done. Then, add a few scale cattle (I added some Preiser 14155 cows), and you have another mini scene on your layout.

Chain link fences

Photo and illustrations by Pelle Søeborg

Pelle Søeborg modified a Walthers Cornerstone kit to create this detailed chain link fence on his HO Daneville Subdivision.

Trackside businesses and industries must protect themselves from theft and vandalism, and chain link fencing is one of the most common ways to provide this type of security. Modeling a chain link fence is a great way to add an interesting detail to a layout. A number of manufacturers make chain link fence kits, including BLMA, Great West Models, Micron Art, and Walthers.

The Walthers HO Cornerstone kit comes with styrene parts for poles, gates, and other details, along with a separate piece of mesh material to simulate the fencing. More recent versions of the kit include 8½" lengths of .019" soft wire, but since I was using an older kit, I had to make some modifications.

After reading the instructions, I thought that following the described assembly method would result in too flimsy a fence. I decided to take an alternative approach.

Instead of gluing the mesh material to the outside of the fence posts as described, I drilled .020" holes through the posts using a no. 76 bit in a pin vise. This is easily done with the posts

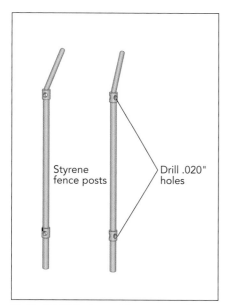

Drill .020" holes with a no. 76 bit at 90 degree angles through the styrene fence posts included in the Walthers kit.

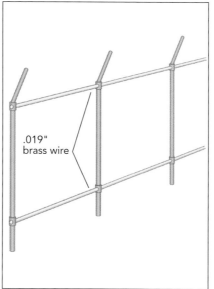

To strengthen the chain link fence, attach the posts to .019" brass wire with CA.

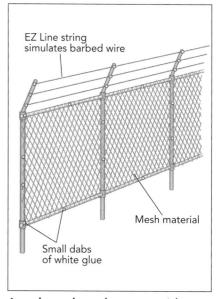

Attach mesh to the posts with white glue. Glue EZ Line to the top of the fence to simulate barbed wire.

still on the sprue. Drill the holes perpendicular to the posts.

Then slide the posts onto the two horizontal wires. I decided against using the styrene rods included in the old Walthers kit for two reasons. First, I needed longer sections of fence than the kit provided. Second, the styrene rods were too soft. I replaced the rods with Detail Associates .019" brass wire (2506), which allowed me to make the fence longer and more stable.

I spaced the posts evenly (the instructions suggest a maximum of 10 scale feet apart) and secured them with cyanoacrylate adhesive (CA). I made hooks for the gates per the instructions.

Next, I glued strips of the mesh to the posts and wire with small dabs of white glue. I find that white glue adheres to almost anything, and it will hold the mesh to both the styrene posts and brass wires. For fence corners, I glued the mesh strips to each side of the corner posts.

The Cornerstone kit lacks the strings of barbed wire sometimes found at the top of chain link fences. To replicate this detail, I used EZ Line from Berkshire Junction (berkshirejunction.com). I glued three strings of EZ Line between each section of the fence using white glue.

Finally, I painted the finished sections of fence with Floquil old silver.

This enamel paint will cause the EZ Line to twist and wrinkle at first, but don't panic. The elastic string will eventually contract to its original position.

Once the paint dried, I was ready to position the chain link fence around the Mills Brothers Lumber warehouse. I drilled 1/32"-diameter holes into the plywood surface and then secured the fence posts in the holes with carpenter's glue.

Thanks to the modifications I made to the kit, I was able to handle the long sections of fence without any damage during installation.

—Pelle Søeborg

Communication poles

Communication line poles, especially if they include the wires, help complete the look of a right-of-way. This HO scene uses Rix poles and EZ Line wires from Berkshire Junction.

Communication lines ran along most railroad rights-of-way from the 1800s through the late 1900s, and they're great details to add to a layout. You can model just the poles themselves, or you can add the wires as well.

These poles carried telegraph and telephone lines, wires for signal communications, and wires to power signals. Poles along a branch line might have a single crossarm with just a few wires, while poles on busy main lines would have three or more crossarms full of wires. By the 1970s, wires and poles began disappearing; however, in many areas, the poles still remain, often without wires or with wires cut and hanging from some poles.

Modelers in HO can use Rix poles, which include separate crossarms. These are beautiful models of the 10-pin arms used by most prototype railroads. Poles by Atlas (HO and N) and Bachmann (N), although commonly available, aren't as good a match for the real thing. However, they can be modified into more realistic models by removing crossarms and insulators.

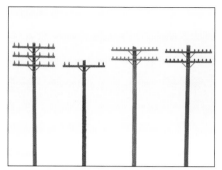

From left: an Atlas HO pole, an Atlas pole trimmed and painted, an unpainted Rix pole, and a painted Rix pole.

Rough up the pole by dragging a razor-saw blade along its length.

You can modify commercial poles by trimming off the top crossarms and removing insulators. This is a Bachmann N scale pole.

Paint poles and crossarms with grimy black, dark brown, and dark gray washes.

Give insulators a base coat of silver. For green insulators, follow with a coat of Testor's jade green enamel paint.

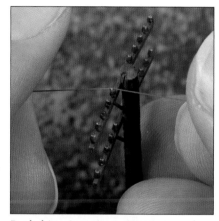

Berkshire Junction's EZ Line works well for modeling wires. Use a toothpick to put a drop of CA atop the insulator and then touch and hold the EZ Line in place for a few seconds.

Real poles have a rough texture, so start by dragging each model pole with the edge of a razor-saw blade. Then modify the poles as needed by trimming away crossarms or removing insulators. Not all insulator positions were used on all poles—see prototype photos for placement ideas.

Next, paint the pole and crossarms. The brown plastic is a good base color, so I like to add washes (one part Polly Scale paint to about five parts water or airbrush thinner) of grimy black and various grays and dark browns.

Insulators on line poles were usually clear or green glass. To represent either type, start by painting each insulator silver using a fine brush. For green

insulators, add a coat of Testor's jade green enamel. It will dry glossy, and the silver undercoat gives it a glass-like sparkle. For clear insulators, follow the silver with a coat of clear gloss finish.

Drill holes in the layout surface to provide a snug fit for the poles. Prototype pole-to-pole spacing was typically 120 to 160 feet, but cutting that down to 90 to 100 feet appears quite realistic on a model railroad. Keep poles on the side of the tracks away from the layout edge. That way, they'll be less likely to be bumped and will also be out of the way when photographing the layout.

For wires, I highly recommend EZ Line from Berkshire Junction, an elastic thread that stretches and returns to

shape if bumped. You can string lines two ways. For the best-looking results, use a toothpick to place a bit of cyanoacrylate adhesive (CA) atop an insulator, pull the EZ Line taut, and then touch the line to the CA for a couple of seconds. This takes a bit of time, especially if you have many wires or a long run.

The easier method is to wrap the line around the base of the insulator and add a drop of CA. The appearance isn't quite as realistic, but if you're doing a lot of wires, the process is much faster, and with multiple wires, it's difficult to notice that the wires are below the insulator unless you really look closely at it.

Diesel number boards

Adding number board decals is an easy way to improve the appearance of many older models, such as these HO scale Kato GP35s.

Number boards are a distinctive feature of diesel locomotives. Most models today come with numbers in place on their number boards, but some older models (or models sold as unnumbered) may not have them. In addition, some factory-installed number boards fall a bit short in the realism department, but they're easy to upgrade.

ShellScale offers a number of decal sets in N, HO, and O scales. These sets are all patterned after specific number styles by a locomotive manufacturer or railroad. Microscale also offers multiple sets in N through O scales.

Adding the number boards is easy. The first step is to add the background decal, which is usually black or white. You can also paint the area, but decals make it easy to get the exact size desired. The Microscale and ShellScale sets include background panels for this, which can be trimmed slightly if needed to fit specific models. A nice touch is that the white background panels usually include black gasket detail as well, as seen on the Illinois Central diesel shown on page 33.

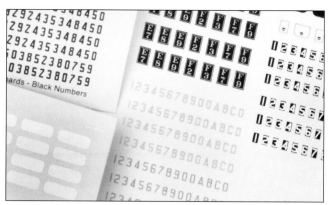

ShellScale (left) and Microscale (right) both offer a variety of number board decal sets in HO, N, and O scales.

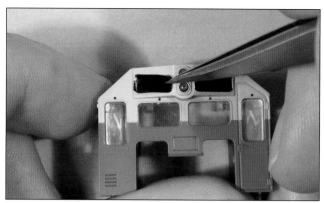

Start by applying the background decal. Add decal setting fluid, such as Micro-Sol, and let it dry completely before adding numerals.

Rio Grande diesels had a nonstandard number style for number boards, captured here by ShellScale decals on an older HO Athearn GP40-2.

The numbers on the steam-style number board of this HO Great Northern Alco RS-2 are from a Microscale alphabet/numeral set.

It's easy to replace factory numbers with decals, as on this HO Proto 2000 E unit.

Use setting solution (such as Microscale Micro-Sol) so the decal settles completely to the surface. Let the background decal dry completely and then apply the numerals one at a time. Allow each one to dry before adding the next to avoid accidentally bumping them out of alignment.

The multitude of available decals allows you to match the style of specific prototypes. The Burlington EMD GP35 diesel shown received standard EMD white numbers (ShellScale HO105). The Rio Grande used a different style on its diesels, as shown by the GP40-2, which received ShellScale HO117 decals. The Great Northern Alco RS-2 had a unique (as far as number boards go) style, which I matched as best as I could with a Microscale block gothic alphabet set (87-123-1).

Sometimes models have numerals in place, but the effect isn't what you need. Maybe the number style isn't an exact match. In the case of the older Proto 2000 E unit, the clear numbers (made to allow backlighting) didn't show up well. This is easy to fix: I simply applied decals (ShellScale HO105) directly over the original number board.

Take a good look at your diesel fleet and look for opportunities to take their number boards to a high level of realism.

Renumber locomotives and cars

These two HO Accurail boxcars originally had the same number. The car on the left had its original number scraped away and a decal added in its place. Weathering helps hide the modification.

Many manufacturers today offer their locomotives and rolling stock with multiple road numbers. However, as modelers expand their fleets, it's easy to wind up with two pieces of equipment having the same number. This can be distracting to operators and viewers, and your layout will have a better overall appearance if duplicate cars are renumbered.

A challenge to removing factory-applied numbers is that manufacturers use different types of paint, so what works for removing lettering from one maker's cars sometimes won't work for another. Also, lettering often isn't paint—it's ink, and the ink lettering can be tougher than the underlying paint.

My favorite method of removing factory-applied numbers is to scrape them off with a hobby knife. Using just

Remove the original numeral by scraping it lightly with a hobby knife and a no. 11 blade. Work slowly and carefully. This is an HO Alco RS-2 from Proto 1000.

The number is gone and the underlying paint is intact, albeit slightly dull from the scraping.

A new decal number, in this case from a Microscale set for Great Northern diesels, is a good match for the factory lettering.

A coat of clear flat finish blends the decal numeral into the rest of the locomotive number.

the tip of a sharp no. 11 blade, held as flat as possible, carefully scrape the number. Go slowly, and don't try to take off too much at once—you want to leave the underlying paint intact. Proceed until the number is gone.

You can then apply a new numeral decal over the removed number. Add a light coat of clear flat finish and a bit of weathering, and the decal will blend well into the original paint scheme.

You'll need to find decals to match the factory lettering. In my examples, I used a Champ set for the Illinois Central boxcar and a Microscale set for the Great Northern diesel. If your decals are a close match in color and style to the car's original numbers, you can get by with replacing a single digit, as with the Great Northern locomotive. However, if the styles don't quite match, you'll get a better

appearance by replacing the entire number, as with the Illinois Central boxcar.

If you remove some underlying paint, don't panic. Touch it up with a fine-point brush and the closest model paint you can find. Matching paint is a tricky process, but you don't have to be exact. As long as you're in the ball-park, a bit of weathering can make your modifications all but invisible.

Freight car markings

Consolidated stencils, ACI labels, and wheel inspection dots can be added to freight cars to set them in the proper era. This HO Accurail model depicts a 1960s-built car in service in the 1980s.

Freight cars offer a number of opportunities for upgrading factory-applied lettering, including consolidated stencils, ACI scanner labels, wheel inspection dots, and hazardous-materials placards. How you use these, and which ones you should add, depends upon the specific time frame you model. A nice variety of decals is available, making these markings easy to add in HO, N, and O scales.

Start by establishing which markings are appropriate for the period you model. Consolidated stencils (often called *lube plates*) are the black squares with white borders found on all modern cars. The panels include information on lubrication dates, inspections and testing, and the build and rebuild dates for the car.

Single-panel stencils first appeared in 1972, with two-panel versions mandated beginning in 1974 (with a target date of 1979 for application on all cars). These changed briefly to a four-panel version (three side-by-side over a narrow panel) in 1982, which was soon changed to three panels (two side-by-side over a narrow panel).

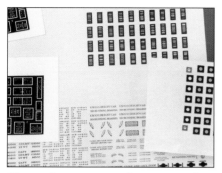

Champ has two sets for one- and two-panel stencils, left, and wheel inspection dots, right. Microscale sets 1 and 2 (center) include ACI labels and one-panel stencils.

Stencils and other decals can be applied directly to factory-painted cars. As with prototype cars, the stencils can cover some original lettering.

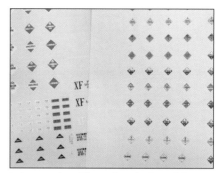

Microscale offers decals for old (left, 228) and new (right, 840) hazardous placards.

Placard decals can be applied directly to the placard holders found on most tank car models.

This old-style DANGEROUS placard is applied to an HO Trix model of an early pressurized tank car in chlorine service.

ACI (automatic car identification) plates are vertical panels with 13 horizontal color stripes. Designed to be read by wayside optical scanners, the panels were introduced in 1967, with a target of 1970 for application to all cars. Grime and weather doomed the system, which was scrapped in 1977. Cars built after that date won't have them, but earlier cars usually retained theirs, often in very weathered condition.

Wheel inspection dots should only appear on cars that were in service from March 1978 through 1980. They indicated that cars had been inspected for a certain manufacturer's defective wheels. Cars without the wheels received a yellow dot; cars with the wheels got a white dot and were in restricted service until the wheels were replaced.

In HO, Microscale (87-1, 87-2, MC-4127) and Champ (HD-31, HD-32) have sets for consolidated stencils (substitute 60- prefix for Microscale's N scale sets). Champ's are for one- and two-panel stencils. Microscale sets 1 and 2 have single-panel stencils and ACI labels. Champ set HD-34 is for HO inspection dots.

Hazardous-material placards are found on tank cars and other cars that haul dangerous cargo. Modern cars include specific information and four-digit product codes, as a result of the Hazardous Materials Transportation Act of 1975. Earlier cars carried more generic placards with lettering such as DANGEROUS or FLAMMABLE.

Apply them in the same manner as you would other decals. I applied a DANGEROUS placard to a Trix HO model of an early high-pressure tank car in chlorine service.

Chalk marks on freight cars

Chalk marks were used by railroads to indicate car routing and switching. This is an HO InterMountain boxcar.

Gel pens can be used to apply chalk marks in HO and larger scales. Use a light touch.

Apply weathering—in this case, some dark gray powdered chalk—between applications of chalk marks.

Sunshine Models offers several sheets of chalk mark decals in HO scale.

This InterMountain car has had several Sunshine decal chalk marks added near the data lettering.

From the steam through early diesel eras, railroad crews relied on chalk marks scrawled on cars for various routing and switching information. These marks can be modeled in several ways. You can apply them directly using a white gel pen or a paint pen. It takes some practice to do this without making the strokes too thick, so practice on an old car or a scrap piece of painted plastic.

A nice touch is to apply one mark and then weather over it before applying another mark. This captures the look of some older chalk marks fading away, with new marks covering them.

Decals are another option. Sunshine Models offers several sets, and each includes dozens of different marks that were all taken from real freight cars. Add these as you would regular decals. Again, weathering between marks enhances the appearance. A coat of clear flat finish will seal the marks and weathering.

Galvanized boxcar roofs

These HO boxcars show paint removed from galvanized roofs, duplicating effects from exposure to the elements.

S ince the 1930s, most boxcar roofs have been made with steel panels riveted or welded together. These panels are galvanized, or coated with zinc, to inhibit rust. Into the 1960s, galvanized roofs were often painted the same color as their boxcar. The paint didn't stick particularly well to the zinc coating, and after a few years of exposure, the paint tended to peel off the panels.

This effect is easy to duplicate by brushing silver paint on roof panels. I use Polly Scale flat aluminum to paint varying sizes of patches on roofs. Newer cars should receive minimal effects, while roofs on a few older cars should be almost devoid of paint. Seam caps (the raised lines between panels) generally retain their paint. Vary the effects among the cars.

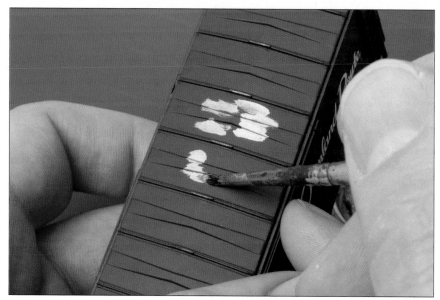

Simply apply flat silver paint in differing patterns to the boxcar roof panels. Finish the cars with a light dusting of gray chalk or a light weathering spray to tone down the silver color and make it look more like galvanized steel.

Model an open boxcar

The wide doors of this Accurail HO boxcar provide a good view of the car's stripwood interior walls, painted and weathered floor, and old packing scraps on the interior.

Boxcars can often be seen rolling along with doors open—either slightly cracked or slid all the way open. Modeling cars in this manner provides an interesting look for a boxcar when in a train or on a siding, but doing it well is a bit more than simply gluing a door in the open position.

You can use any sliding-door (not plug-door) boxcar. I started with an HO Accurail 50-foot boxcar lettered for Gulf, Mobile & Ohio.

Seeing into an open car means you'll be able to view the interior walls and floor. Most general-purpose boxcars have wood interior walls, either plank or plywood. Red Caboose offers several HO and O scale laser-cut interior wall kits with peel-and-stick backing; you can use one of these, but since I didn't have one on hand, I simply used thin stripwood (1/32" thick) stained with thinned grimy black paint (one part Polly Scale grimy black to eight parts Polly S Airbrush Thinner).

I didn't apply the strips all the way to the end, figuring it would be difficult to see more than a scale 15 feet

I stained stripwood pieces and glued them to the boxcar's interior walls with CA.

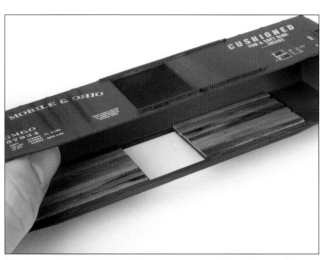

The interior walls don't have to extend to the end—just make sure they cover the normal viewing range.

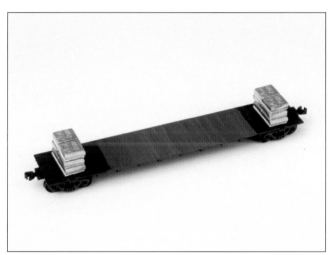

Paint and weather the floor where it will be visible. The A-Line peel-and-stick weights will be out of sight on each end.

This InterMountain HO boxcar received a Jaeger grain door. Its torn appearance means the car is ready to be cleaned out and reloaded.

or so into the car. I added drops of cyanoacrylate adhesive (CA) along the length of a board and then placed the board on the wall. I started at the bottom at the floor. Keep applying boards until you reach the top.

I painted the floor to represent wood in the same way Lou Sassi paints a flatcar deck on pages 92–93: first painting the floor grimy black and then painting individual boards various shades of brown and light and dark gray.

To replace the floor-length, sheet-metal weight that came with the kit, I used 1.5 ounces of A-Line peel-and-stick weights at each end of the floor, which will remain well out of normal viewing range.

I finished the car by adding some scrap material to the floor that might have been left after unloading: a couple of wood scraps and a few cut-apart cardboard cases.

As another example of an open-door car, I modeled an InterMountain boxcar to represent a recently unloaded grain car. I used a Red Caboose interior in this car, painted the floor, and then weathered it with yellow chalk to represent dust remaining from a grain load.

The Signode grain door is from Jaeger (2000). I glued the door in place inside the door opening with CA and then tore it fully along one side and partially along the other, wrinkled it, and pushed it back inside. It could be waiting to be cleaned on a yard track or waiting to travel back to grain country for reloading.

To find other examples of how you can model open-door cars, watch for real-life cars and look at prototype photos.

Weather models with chalk

These N scale Micro-Trains freight cars have all received chalk weathering on their bodies and trucks.

Weathering with chalk is one of the easiest and quickest methods of giving locomotives and rolling stock the appearance that they've been working hard in the real world.

Several manufacturers offer powdered chalk in weathering colors ready to use, including AIM Products (1103100) and Bar Mills (45). You can also use artist's pastel chalks, scraping the chalk with a knife to get powder as you need it. The chalks can be blended to create a wide variety of colors.

A key to success with chalk weathering is to apply it to models painted with flat paints. Chalks simply do not stick well to gloss and semigloss surfaces, especially if you try to seal them

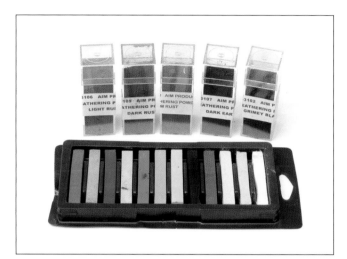

AIM Products offers powdered chalk in several weathering colors. You can also use artist's pastel chalks.

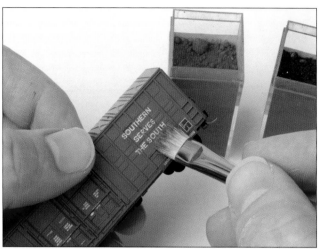

Use a stiff brush to apply grimy streaks on the sides, ends, and roofs of models.

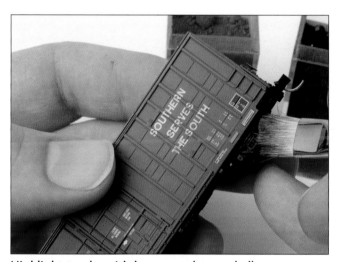

Highlight trucks with brown and gray chalk.

Chalk works well for simulating exhaust residue on diesel locomotive roofs.

with an overspray of clear finish. If a model has a glossy surface, give it a light coat of clear flat (from an airbrush or spray can) before applying chalk.

Black and various shades of gray work well for giving rolling stock a general grimy appearance. Using a stiff brush (such as hog bristle) makes it easy to create a streaked look as it grinds the chalk into the paint surface.

Simulate faded lettering and paint by brushing on chalk that matches the car color. I did this with the Milwaukee Road car shown. The color doesn't have to be an exact match to get a good effect.

Chalk also is effective in adding rust and grime colors to trucks and for modeling exhaust residue on locomotive roofs and sides. I find a soft brush works well for these applications—you

don't want any brush marks, just an overall dusted, grimy appearance.

It's a good idea to seal the effects by adding a light overspray of clear flat finish. I prefer Polly Scale Flat Finish applied with an airbrush or Testor's Model Master Lusterless Clear (1960) from a spray can. Use a light coat and your weathering should stay intact. You can also add a second application of chalk if needed.

Weather freight car trucks

Weathering freight car trucks includes painting the sideframes, highlighting details such as the red roller-bearing adapters and springs, and painting the wheel faces. This is an HO InterMountain covered hopper on roller-bearing trucks.

Trucks are easy to overlook when weathering a freight car. But they are certainly worthy of attention and can add an extra level of detail to a model.

There are two basic types of trucks: solid bearing and roller bearing. Most early trucks (through the 1960s) were solid bearing (often called friction bearing). The end bearings of these trucks' axles were covered by a journal box. The lid on the journal box opened, allowing oil to be added to cotton fiber waste that lubricated

the bearing. These required frequent lubrication.

Since the 1960s, roller-bearing trucks have been required on all new equipment, and solid-bearing trucks have been banned from interchange service since the mid-1990s. Roller bearings are sealed, don't require lubrication, and are more free-rolling than solid bearings. The trucks are distinctly different, with bearing end caps that rotate with the wheels.

To weather either type of truck, start by painting the sideframes with

This HO Accurail boxcar received some detail upgrades including Kato ASF Ride Control trucks. The sideframes are painted grimy black with rust highlights on the springs and journal box. The wheel faces are painted with black and oily black.

By adding paints, such as grimy black and dark brown, to an old film-container (or similar) lid, you can mix colors while painting the truck sideframes.

Highlight detail areas on the sideframes. Here, the roller-bearing adapters receive a bit of boxcar red paint.

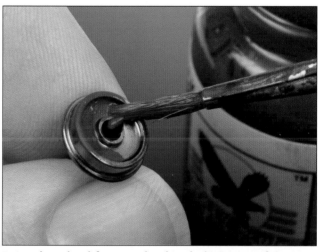

Paint the wheel faces with a brush, being careful not to get paint on the needlepoint axle bearings.

an airbrush or brush. Real trucks most often start out black (some railroads paint them to match the cars), but they quickly weather to a grimy black or brown color. I start with Polly Scale grimy black, often mixing in railroad tie brown to vary the shade.

Highlight truck components with appropriate colors. Roller bearing adapters (which rest just above the end caps) are often dark red, and some newer end caps are blue. Journal box covers can show signs of rust or oil—use a brush or chalk to highlight this.

You can also streak a bit of rust on the springs or other components.

Prototype wheels are unpainted. New wheels are often a light orange-brown rust color, and on roller-bearing trucks, they tend to become progressively darker over time, turning dark brown to grimy black. Wheels on solid-bearing trucks often picked up oil from the journal boxes over time, becoming black with a textured, oily appearance.

Metal wheelsets have several advantages over plastic ones. Their treads stay cleaner, and they help keep track

clean, lower a car's center of gravity, and look better than plastic wheelsets. If a car has plastic wheels, I swap in a pair of InterMountain, Kadee, or Reboxx replacement wheelsets.

Use a brush to paint wheel faces, starting with Polly Scale grimy black, rust, or railroad tie brown. I paint some wheels on solid-bearing trucks with engine black or oily black. Make sure you don't get any paint on the needle-point axle ends.

Pop the wheelsets into the trucks and your cars are ready to hit the rails.

Add rust with oil paint

Light rust, heavy rust, and chalked-lettering effects are easy to replicate using artist's oil colors. These are HO scale InterMountain cars.

Freight cars weather in many different ways depending upon their age and exposure to the elements. On older cars, it is common to see rusted areas high on the body with rust-colored stains running downward. This is an easy effect to duplicate in any scale.

You can use artist's oil paints to create this effect. Get small tubes of burnt sienna, raw sienna, and raw umber. Mixing these paints gives you an infinite variety of light to dark rust colors. An advantage of using oil paints is that they give you a lot of working time, so if the effect isn't what you want, a cloth dipped in turpentine removes it and you can start over.

Begin by squeezing dabs of each color on a scrap piece of styrene. Use a small brush to make rust patches. Rust patches often occur on the roof,

Paint rust patches in various colors on the car side. The oil paint gives the rust some texture as well as color.

Wet a wide, flat brush with turpentine and streak it along the car side from top to bottom.

To simulate chalked, streaked lettering, paint over the lettering with white oil paint.

Streak the damp brush over the lettering to create the weathered effect.

the seam where the roof meets the body, boxcar door tracks, places where the car has been bumped or scraped, ladder and grab iron mounting points, and areas where lettering has chipped away.

Wet a wide, soft artist's brush with turpentine. (For easy use, pour a little bit in an old jar lid.) Drag the brush smoothly down the car side to create streaks. To vary the appearance, repeat the process using different amounts of turpentine on the brush as this will create different effects.

You can also use this technique to capture the look of lettering that is chalking and streaking down the car side. First, paint over the letters with white oil paint. You don't have to be precise. Then, using a wide, soft artist's brush, go over the paint with turpentine to complete the effect.

The streaked areas will dry fairly quickly, but the rust patches can take a day or two to dry. Set the car aside and avoid touching the weathered areas. When the paint has dried, give the car a light overcoat of flat finish (using an airbrush or spray can) to seal the effects.

You can use this technique for light rust, as on the Spokane, Portland & Seattle car, or for heavy rust, as on the Monon car.

Weather a flatcar deck

Photos by Lou Sassi

Forney No. 8 sports a newly painted and weathered flatcar at the Forster Toothpick Mill in Strong, Maine, on Lou Sassi's On2½ layout. Lou used a simple technique to make the plastic flatcar deck look like weather-beaten wood.

I have some Bachmann wood-deck flatcars that I use on my On2½ Sandy River & Rangeley Lakes RR. These models are well detailed and include molded-in planks and wood grain on the deck. However, the deck is the same Tuscan Red color as the flatcar's body, which doesn't quite capture the gray, weather-beaten look of a prototype wood deck. The quick and easy weathering techniques I used on the flatcar can also be applied to other simulated wood surfaces.

After having my good friend George Micklus paint and letter the flatcars for the SR&RL, I went to work making the plastic decks look more like wood. Using acrylic paints and powered artist's pastels, I finished the project in an evening.

I began by brush-painting the deck of each car with Polly Scale Reefer Gray. As soon as the base coat had dried to the touch, I used a no. 0 brush to paint individual boards at random. I first applied Polly Scale D&H Gray and then New Gravel Gray.

After the paint had dried, I used a stiff oil-painting brush to apply black and gray shades of Weber-Costello

Begin the weathering by brush-painting a base coat of Polly Scale Reefer Gray on the flatcar deck. Then paint random boards with Polly Scale D&H Gray and New Gravel Gray.

After the paint has dried, weather the deck with shades of black, gray, and brown powdered artist's pastel chalks.

The finished flatcar (top) looks a lot more realistic than the freshly painted model. You can also use this technique to effectively weather simulated wood structures.

Hi-Fi Gray pastels, followed by two or three of the darker brown earth tones. These pastels come in sticks, so I scraped a hobby knife along each stick to form a powder that I could apply with a brush.

If you want, you can secure the pastels with a light application of Testor's Dullcote. However, it will take longer to weather the deck because you'll have to reapply dry colors each time the Dullcote is applied. Dullcote has a tendency to visually dissipate the powders. On this project, I didn't bother with the Dullcote application since I don't handle my equipment enough to warrant that step.

In the above photo, you can see the dramatic results of the finished, detailed flatcar compared to the out-of-the-box model. By completing this simple project, you can easily improve the look of your model flatcar fleet.

—*Lou Sassi*

Realistic hopper loads

This HO Walthers car was given a new ore load on a piece of foam core carved to the proper shape. The technique is easy and can be done in any scale.

Hoppers and gondolas carry a variety of loads including coal, iron ore, and crushed rock and other aggregates. Many model railcars don't include loads, or they come with molded loads that often fall short on realism. Adding new loads is an easy project that greatly improves the appearance of hoppers and other cars.

If a car includes a molded load, the first step is to remove it. A fine screwdriver can be used to free the load, but be careful not to damage the car while doing it.

If the load has the proper shape (as with New York Central hopper shown on the opposite page) but an unrealistic color or texture, it can be used as a base for the new load. Set it aside for now.

To make a base for a new load, cut a piece of foam core to the shape of car. It should fit just snug enough to lightly rub the sides and ends when inserted. You may have to carve the bottom-side ends at an angle, so the base rests properly on the hopper's slope sheets.

Use a hobby knife to carve the top of the foam core to the rough shape of the load. This usually means crowned down

These N scale Micro-Trains cars have great detail, but their molded aggregate and coal loads aren't very realistic.

Loads can generally be removed with a bit of "persuasion" from a flat screwdriver. Just be careful not to mar the model.

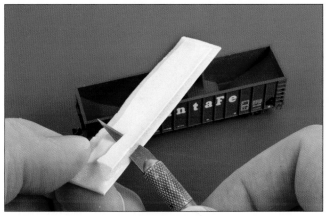

Cut a new load base from foam core and then carve the top to the rough shape of the load.

Brush the base with a heavy coat of paint—Polly Scale engine black for this N scale coal load.

Sprinkle a heavy coat of scale coal over the paint and press the material firmly in place with a finger.

The Santa Fe and Chessie cars have new loads on foam core, while the NYC hopper received a layer of scale coal.

the middle and sloping toward the sides and ends. The edges should rest at least a scale foot below the tops of the car sides.

Tape the load to a piece of scrap that you can use as a handle and then give the top a heavy coat of paint that's close to the load color, such as black for a coal load. This also applies to loads that you're reusing.

While the paint is wet, sprinkle the new load material onto the paint. I do this in a shoebox lid, so it is easy to recover unused material. I used scale coal from Highball Products for the coal loads, Woodland Scenics fine iron ore ballast in the ore car, and Woodland

Scenics fine gray blend ballast for the aggregate car.

Use a finger to press the material firmly into the wet paint. Let the load sit until the paint is dry and then shake any loose material back into its package. Place the finished loads into their cars, and they're ready to hit the rails.

More ideas for a better-looking layout

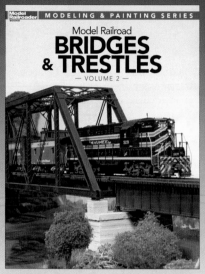

MODELING & PAINTING SERIES

Model Railroad
BRIDGES & TRESTLES
— VOLUME 2 —

Add authenticity to your layout by learning how to model a highway underpass, build a viaduct, create a stone arch bridge, and more. Scratchbuilding tips for customizing your own structures are also included.

#12474 • $17.95

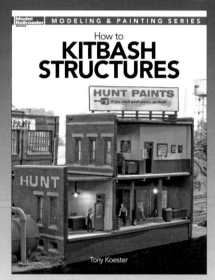

MODELING & PAINTING SERIES

How to
KITBASH STRUCTURES

Tony Koester

Add more personality to your model railroad with kitbashed structures. Respected modeler **Tony Koester** provides many examples of modified kits, including railroad buildings, lineside industries, coal tipples, storefronts, and more.

#12472 • $21.95

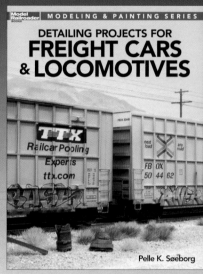

MODELING & PAINTING SERIES

DETAILING PROJECTS FOR
FREIGHT CARS & LOCOMOTIVES

Pelle K. Søeborg

Achieve amazing realism for your locomotives and rolling stock by learning **Pelle Søeborg's** weathering and detailing techniques. He'll teach you how to add rust to a steel coil car, weather black locomotives and white reefers, use pot scrubbers to make a scrap metal load, and more.

#12477 • $19.95

Buy now from hobby shops! To find a store near you, visit www.HobbyRetailer.com

www.KalmbachStore.com or call 1-800-533-6644

Monday – Friday, 8:30 a.m. – 4:30 p.m. CST. Outside the United States and Canada call 262-796-8776, ext. 661.

P19613

KALMBACH BOOKS

2XMR